AF479205

Light of Touch

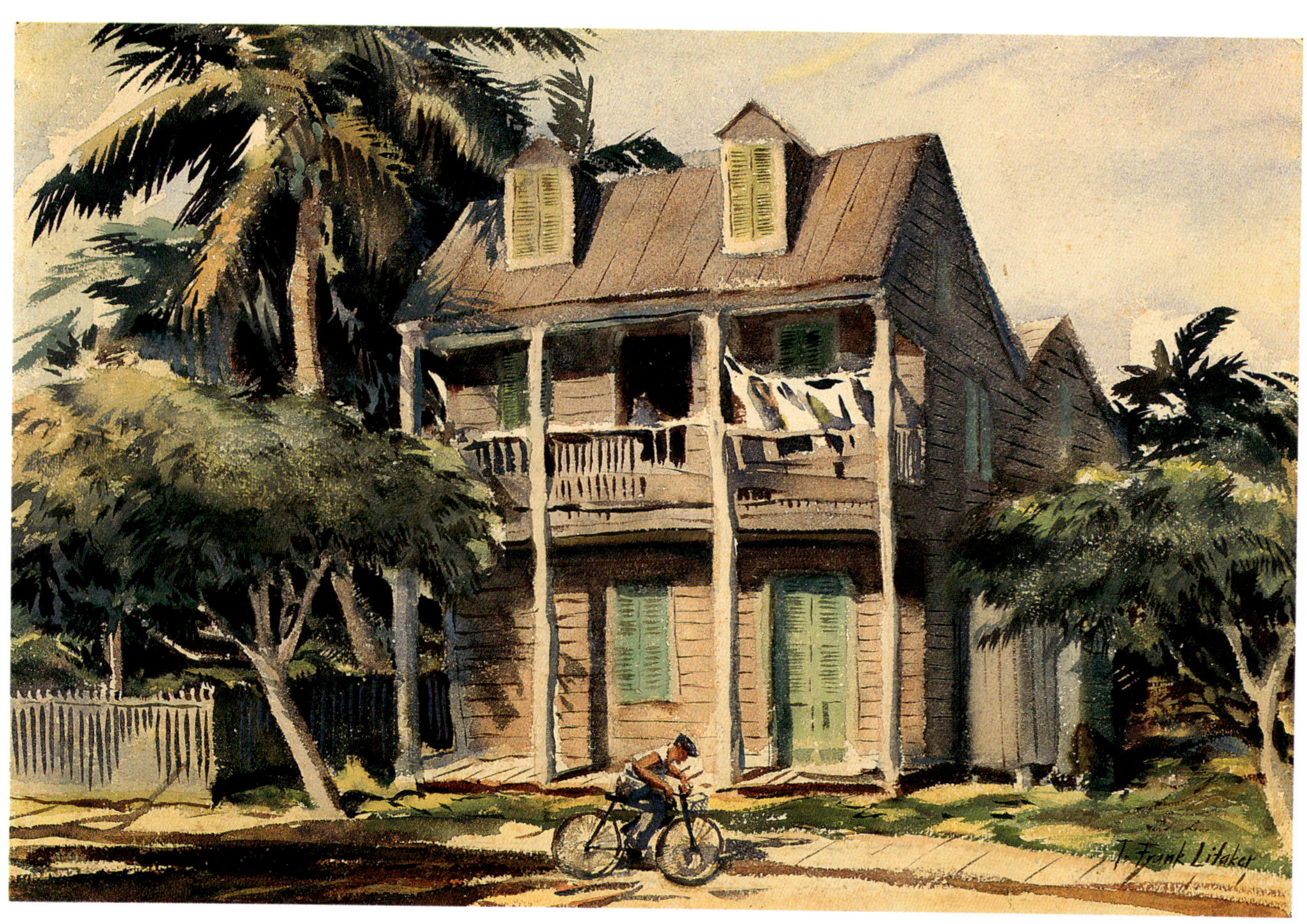

T. Frank Litaker

Coastal Home with Bicyclist

Watercolor on paper, 13 x 19 inches
1993.CO271

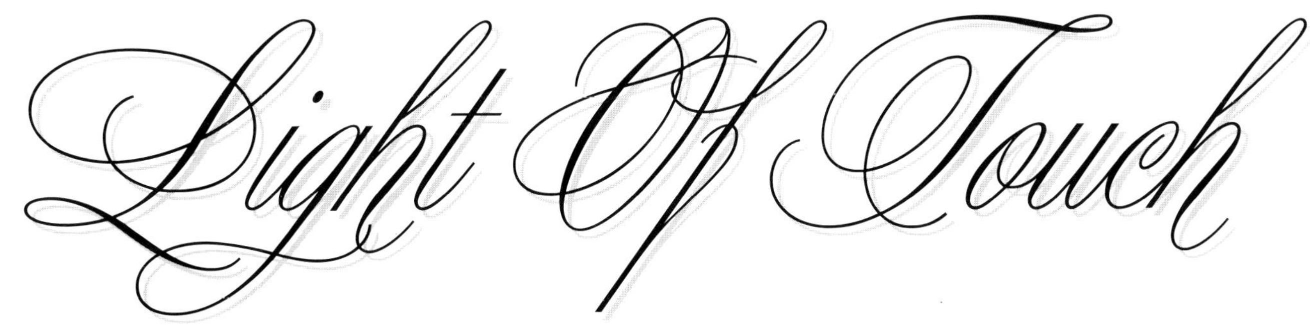

Select Works on Paper
from the Permanent Collection
of the Morris Museum of Art

ESTILL CURTIS PENNINGTON

Curator of Southern Painting

with a foreword by

WILLIAM S. MORRIS III

Chairman of the Board of Trustees

MORRIS MUSEUM OF ART · AUGUSTA GEORGIA

*The author would like to gratefully acknowledge the
aid, patience and assistance of Louise Keith Claussen,
Catherine Wahl, Kevin Strickland, Patrick Taylor,
Jeff Barnes and Lydia Inglett in the preparation of
this work.*

BOOK DESIGN AND TYPOGRAPHY: Jeff Level

ISBN 0-9638753-0-2

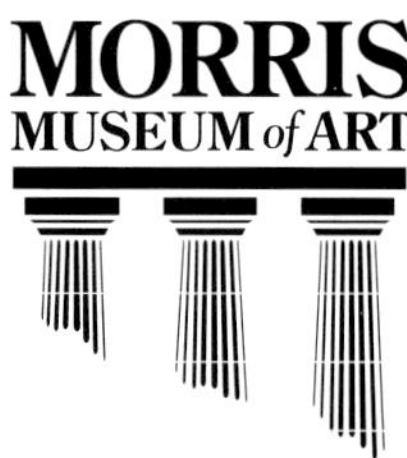

MORRIS MUSEUM OF ART

One 10th Street

Augusta Georgia 30901-1134

706.724.7501

MCMXCIII

Contents

George L. Viavant

1872 – 1925

Meadowlark

1914

Watercolor on paper, 16⅝ x 10¾ inches
1989.01.214

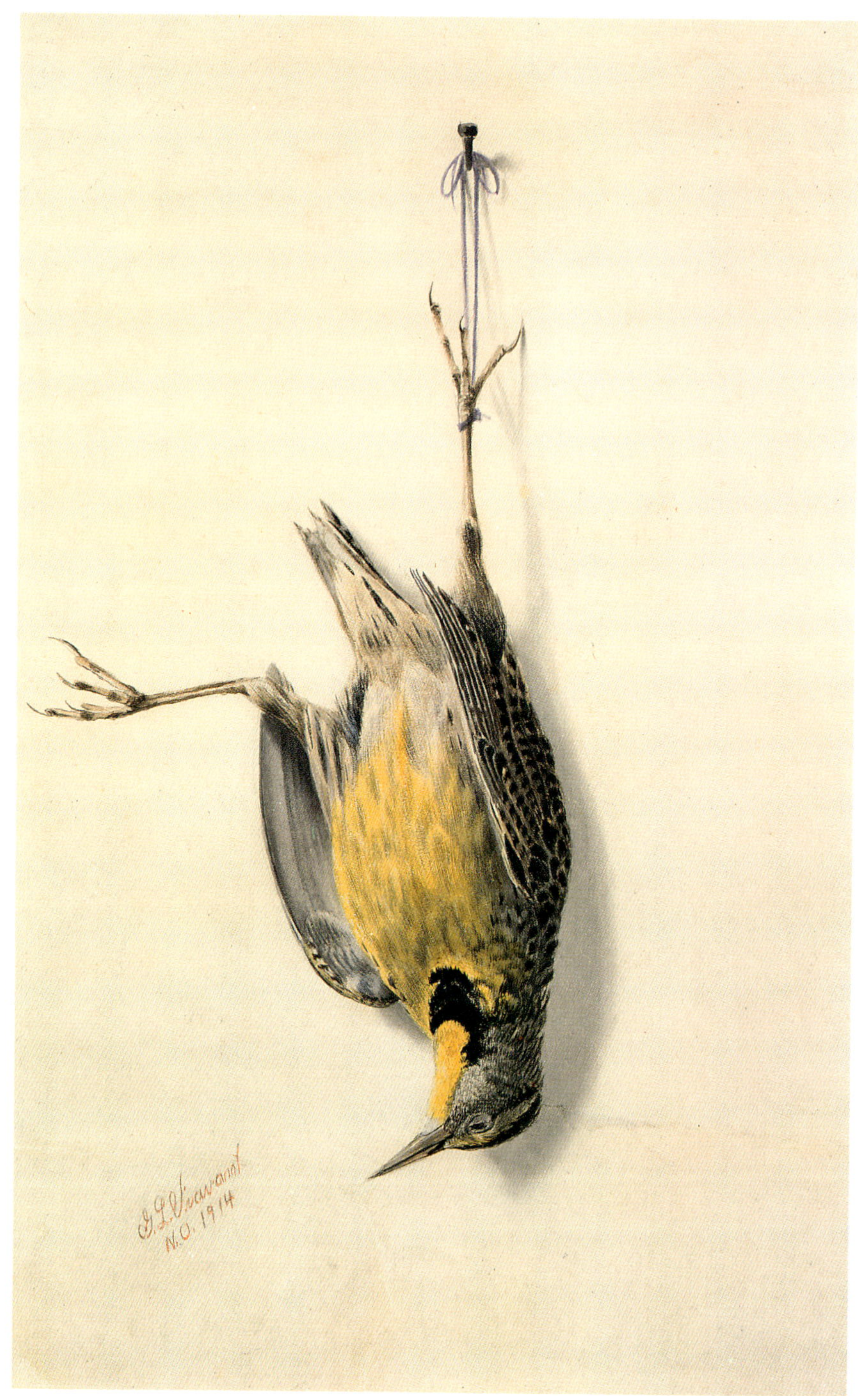

Foreword

Among the earliest images in the history of the South are works on paper —
maps, naturalistic studies, botanical sketches – created by artists who, with the material
at hand, captured their first impressions of the new world.

Some of the oldest works in the Morris Museum of Art's collection are works on
paper. John Abbot's delicate watercolors of birds, for example, date to 1790. Works on
paper, however are not confined to historical images, and the museum's collection
includes a number of watercolors, drawings and pastels executed by contemporary
Southern artists.

With the acquisition of an extensive body of art collected by the late Dr. Robert
Powell Coggins, the Morris Museum of Art became the repository for a large number
of works on paper relating to the South. These works range from wildlife sketches by
the early American naturalists to finely drawn portraits to watercolor impressions of
the lush Southern landscape.

In this volume, the Morris Museum of Art seeks to document works on paper
from a broad range of art in the South. "Light of Touch" is not intended to be a
comprehensive study; a wealth of material remains to be explored and presented.
Rather, it is an introduction to some 41 representative works in the collection,
arranged chronologically according to the date they were created.

In his essay, Morris Museum of Art Curator of Southern Painting Estill Curtis
Pennington touches on the special quality of works on paper – works which, by their
very nature, are tied to a particular moment in time, a particular feeling, a momentary
vision. And, as is often the case with Southern art in general, there are strong links to
Southern literature. These drawings and watercolors have a sense of immediacy, that
direct, personal quality which is most appropriate for a Southern collection.

The Morris Museum of Art is pleased to present these works on paper, and thus
to inspire further exploration in a singularly fascinating area of Southern art history.

– William S. Morris III
Chairman of the Board of Trustees

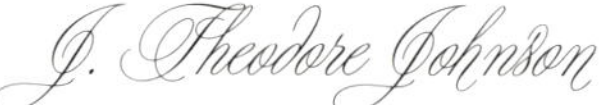

J. Theodore Johnson

b. 1902

Woman Seated at Open Window

c. 1925

Watercolor on paper, 11½ x 9 inches
1993.C1394

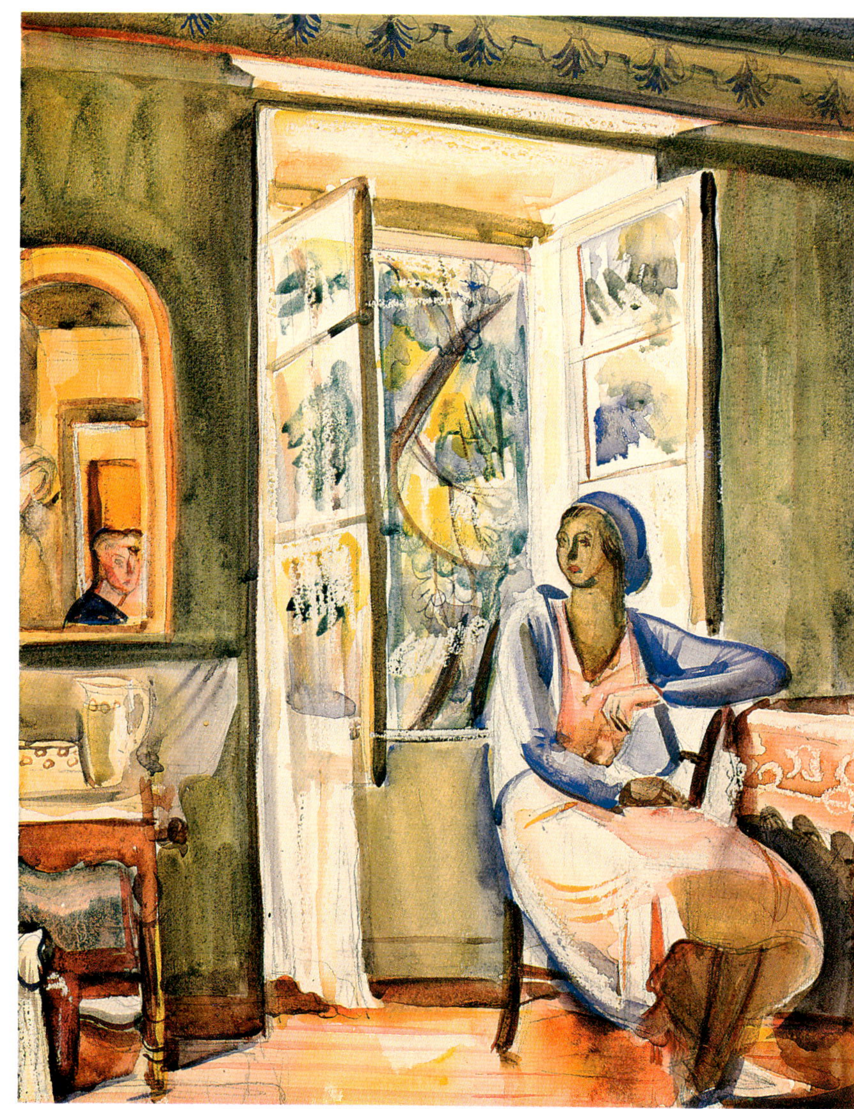

Like a letter lost and found many years later, J. Theodore Johnson's watercolor imparts an intriguing message. Inscriptions on the mat surrounding the work, in a hand which matches that of the signature, would seem to indicate Johnson painted this scene while on a trip to the deep South in the mid-1930s. Johnson, then a Chicago-based artist, spent very little time in the South, and is often identified with Southern California where he lived and taught after the Second World War. What then, does this work really have to do with the South?

The image abounds with well-planted clues. A palmetto border runs around the top of the walls, one of several details that give the room a very solid sense of definition. Through the tall, open veranda doors we seem to look out upon a garden beyond. On closer examination we can see that this is a self-portrait, the artist looking with a gawky, quizzical stare into a mirror which casts his reflection before our very eyes, so that we, too, have been let into this scene.

And what of the scene itself? A black model sits gracefully in a chair before the window, posing for the artist with great calm. Her attitude is that of a Renaissance madonna, head slightly tilted to one side in a vaguely Byzantine manner, her figure in a curving parallel to the picture plane, her arm extended in a quiet baroque gesture of composed welcome.

Altogether, one has the sense of looking in upon a scene of much greater importance than a chance studio encounter. The warmth and brilliance of the colors evoke the heat and light of a deep South summer. That the model is an African-American reminds us of an ancient conundrum in the art of the South – black models painted by white artists in an effort to create an exotic air. The artist as outsider portraying an elegant sitter from a sub-culture is a frequent interaction enhancing the entire fabric of Southern life.

This is also a work which reveals the extent to which works of art in general, and works on paper in particular, can convey the mood and atmosphere of certain moments in time and space. The fleeting, tentative quality of the brush or the pencil results in visual objects with a more vulnerable nature, a lightness of touch unseen in the solidity of an oil painting or the deceptive reality of a photograph.

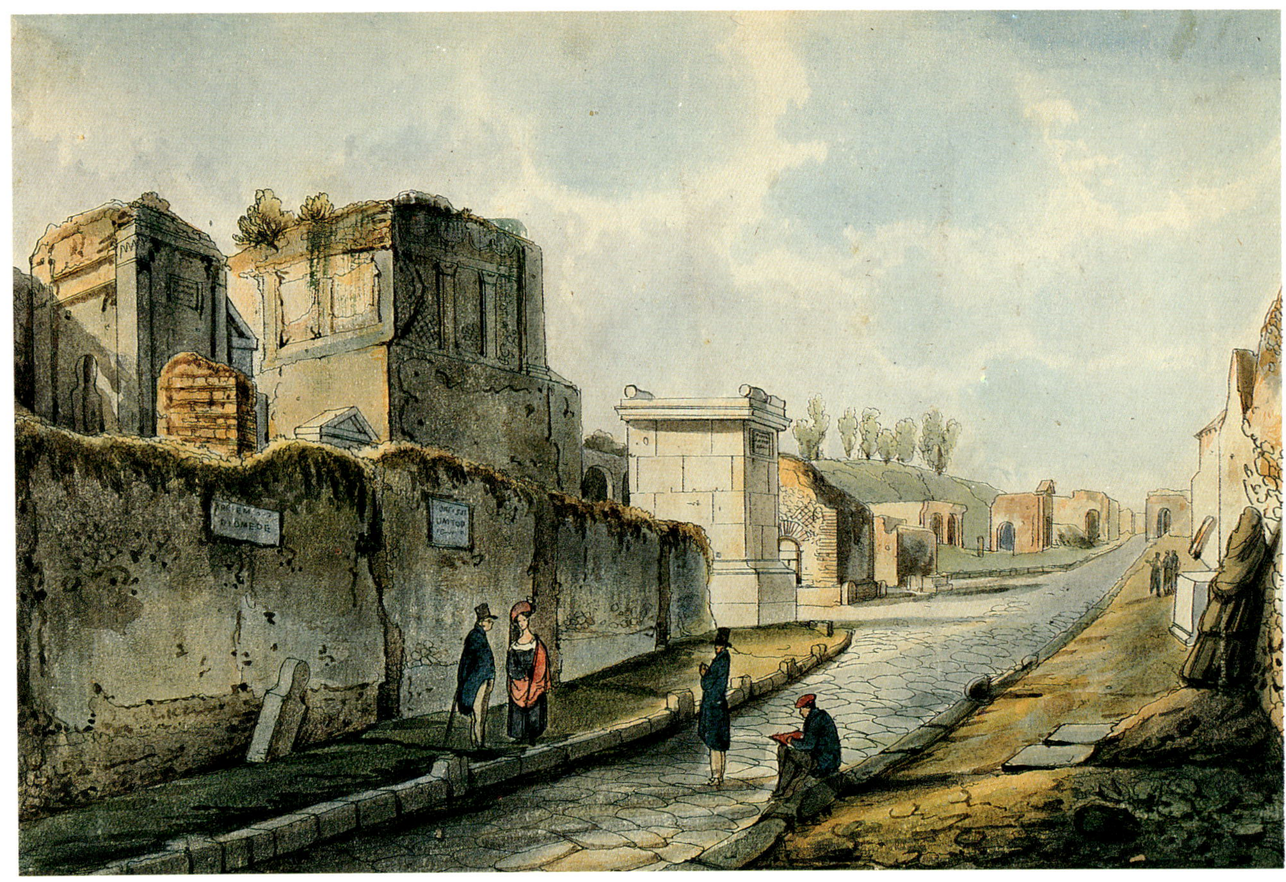

James Hamilton Shegogue

1806 – 1872

Visitors at the Ruins

Watercolor on paper, 5 ⅜ x 7 ⅝ inches
1993.CSB52

Experiencing that moment is immediate and reflective. On the immediate level we 'see' what is before us, but upon reflection we may recall a vast array of historical and cultural associations expanding our understanding of the work as far more illustrative of instance than simple exposition.

In Johnson's watercolor, we are, somewhat like Alice, on the other side of the looking glass, peering into a room from which we can also see out. The view brings to mind a recurring theme in Southern literature, that moment when the young protagonist realizes that youth is over, dispelled by a sudden confrontation with a sobering aspect of the past that is disturbing, but inevitable, as idealism and hope merge with that first hesitant understanding of the complexity of life itself. Maturity follows.

Many of the works in this catalog are from that very moment in time which the writers of the South, in the middle years of this century, captured with such brilliance and insight. From this vantage we are compelled to question whether that same burst of energy which characterizes the writers of the Southern literary renascence, working from the early 1920s through the 1960s, also typifies the spirit of Southern artists working in the same time. In many ways it is now a time as remote to the cultural life of the South as the antebellum period. It was a time when the presence of a mannered past, recalled in the oral tradition, and the importance of place as a locus of the imagination, were potent central themes.

It is critically important to recall that those writers and artists worked in an era when various aspects of American culture had not been homogenized by mass media, nor had the widespread mobility of peoples re-inhabited the South, forever changing the cultural patterns of place. Until the second world war the South may have been the most remote place in America. The South had not shared in the widespread prosperity of the industrial Northeast and Midwest. The agricultural prosperity of the West was not tainted with poverty and depleting land use as in the South.

And, at that point, the South still had a real past, a past rife with political crises and racial conflict, a past which had not yet been made into movies and books that trivialized its reality even as it vividly conveyed its metaphors. That sense of the past is now gone from the South; our popular culture is more at one with that of the nation at large. But certain works of art endure which capture that lost time with beauty, and with a gentle pathos colored by the light of the day of creation. Art can become a lens though which we glimpse the spirit of a place which is no more.

William Alexander Percy, in his book *Lanterns on the Levee,* intones a classic lament for the passing of the unique character of Southern life. "My generation, inured to doom, wears extinction with a certain wry bravado, but it is just as well the older ones we loved are gone. They had lived, for the most part, through tragedy into poverty, which can be and usually is accomplished with dignity and a certain fine disdain."

It was that fine disdain which Rosa Coldfield, in William Faulkner's novel, *Absalom, Absalom,* conveyed to the young Quentin Compson as they sat "in a dim hot airless room with the blinds all closed and fastened. . . ." It was the same disdain the young hero of Truman Capote's novella, *Other Voices, Other Rooms,* felt when he looked up toward the second floor window of the house sinking ever deeper into a symbolic mire of deception and conceit, and saw the sad old lady of the South dancing before the tattered curtains. Ultimately, it is the mendacity of which Tennessee Williams writes so often, people held hostage to dreams and illusions.

Art is an illusion, projecting a symbolic reality drawn from personal experience. While on the grand tour, James Hamilton Shegogue, an artist from Charleston, captured with considerable charm, the ruins of Rome. Shegogue was a product of the golden age of art in Charleston, in the early nineteenth century when portraiture and history painting dominated taste.

In the absence of photography he paused to sketch his own souvenirs, absorbing Italian drawing lessons in the process. Like other Southern artists who were his contemporaries, notably Thomas Sully and William Edward West, he found his return to the old world instructive, a means of reclaiming one cultural heritage and using it to transform provincial inspiration into accomplished expression.

Transformation is one of the most apparent stylistic vehicles in the works on paper in this collection. An artist transforms what he sees by the technique and style he practices. Style and taste change, moving, it often seems, in cycles of exuberance and restraint, reminding us of specific interests at now remote moments. Artists practice transformation when they appropriate recurring visual motifs, investing them with new meaning, achieving an impact other than that originally intended.

A case in point may be seen in the still-life art of George L. Viavant. Although Charles Fraser and William Aiken Walker both practiced a form of trompe l'oeil still-life art with their hanging game pictures, it was really George L. Viavant of New Orleans who mastered the technique and created some of the finest efforts in the genre. Viavant was a product of the best developed art training available in the South at the time. As a student of Achille Perelli at the Southern Art Union in New Orleans, Viavant learned to draw from casts and from life, a discipline he pursued with the Italian-born master for nine years.

In 1884 Viavant enjoyed considerable success with an exhibition of his work at the Cotton Exposition in New Orleans. Thereafter, gallery sales and commissions kept him sufficiently busy to pursue his artwork full time. In 1889 he moved to the family plantation on Bayou Sauvage, Gentilly. An undated local news feature from the period notes that this spot, "nestled amidst giant magnolias and towering pecan trees, whence is wafted the fragrant perfume of the sweet olive and orange blossoms, far from the hurry and bustle of modern New Orleans, the artist naturalist brings forth his master works."

Was Viavant really a naturalist? Certainly John James Audubon, who was possessed by a compulsive desire to record all the species of birds in North America, was a kind of naturalist. Audubon belongs to an eighteenth-century tradition of sublime appreciation of the natural world, of whose wonders he ever stood in awe. Viavant's art is part of the late nineteenth-century belief in the ultimate ability of man to triumph over nature.

Audubon's works depict birds in the wild, or in local settings. Though sometimes awkwardly rendered, they are presented as living creatures. Viavant paints them hanging lifeless from a nail in an anonymous wall. However realistically they are depicted, they are indeed still life, *nature mort*. . . nature dead.

Elizabeth Connell, writing of Viavant's contemporary William Michael Harnett, views nature mort as having a "certain late Victorian penchant for reflection and reveries. . . evoked in the dark tonalities and precisely detailed accounts of age and war." Viavant's art is an art that celebrates the harvest of wild game, an affirmation of prosperity, abundance, the triumph of progress initiated by the industrial revolution and fulfilled in the surging movement west.

But in keeping with the cycles of art, many in this century have rediscovered the wilderness, transforming near-forgotten flora and fauna in the more remote swamps and bayous of the South into new art expressions. Anna Heyward Taylor of South Carolina was one of the artists who renewed and transformed the botanic art field.

Taylor gives the impression of having seized every opportunity open to her, enriching both her life and art in very individual ways. Her family's means made it possible for her to attend Radcliffe College and to study abroad with William Merritt Chase in England and Holland before the First World War. During the war she was an ambulance driver for the Red Cross and remained active in that organization throughout her life.

In 1916 and again in 1920 she accompanied the naturalist William Beebe on his expedition to British Guiana where she sketched and painted the local flora. Upon her return she conveyed these drawings to the medium of batik, mastering the paint and wax process. Within the next few years she also became a highly proficient printmaker in the linoleum block medium.

Taylor's extensive travels, and her willingness to experiment with medium and subject matter, combined with her keenly observant eye, give her version of the Carolina low country a personal, expressionistic spirit. The broad scale and sweep of her azaleas dominate the leafy swamps around them. The passing white heron in flight adds a dashing note.

It is interesting to compare the efforts of Taylor with those of Alice Smith, both as artists of the Charleston Renaissance and as women artists seeking self-expression in a landscape they clearly loved. Smith's work is about the mystery of nature, and the subliminal beauty which resides there, waiting to be detected in glorious passages of light and shadow.

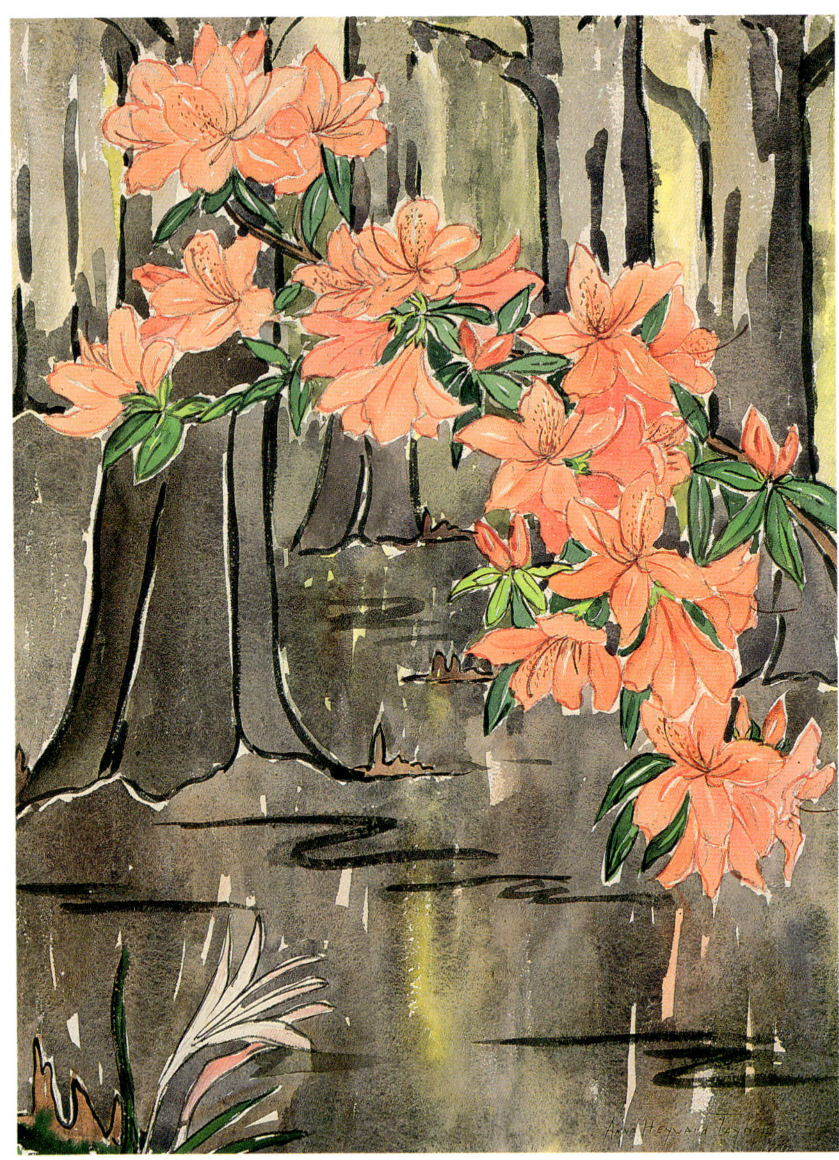

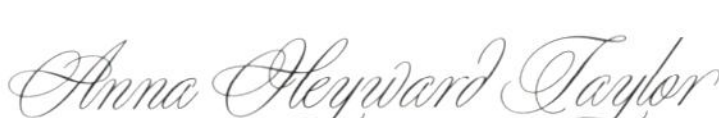
Anna Heyward Taylor

1879 – 1956

Swamp Azaleas

1920

Watercolor on paper, 22 x 16 inches
1989.01.203

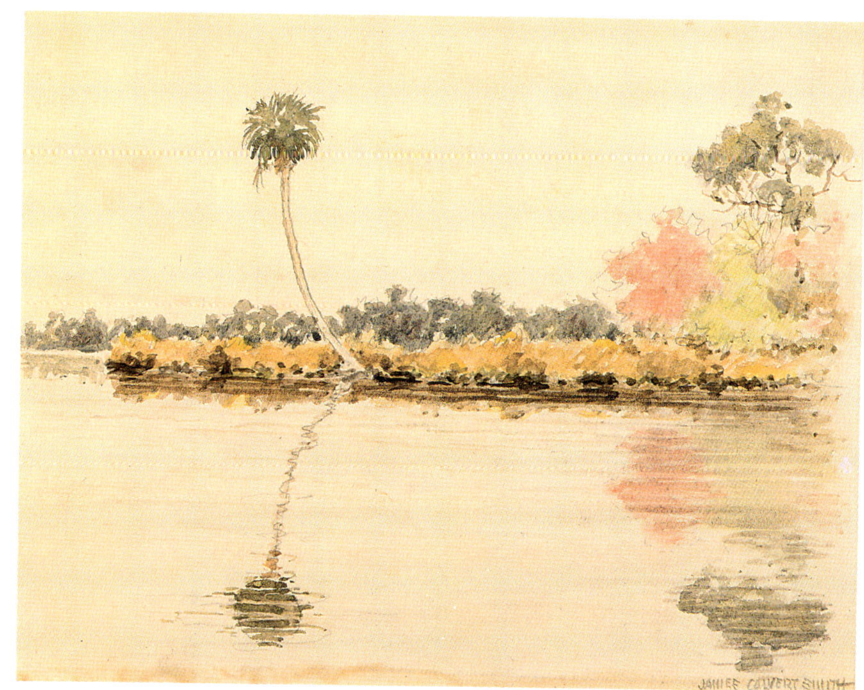

James Calvert Smith

1878 – 1962

Waterway, Florida

c. 1940

Watercolor and graphite on paper,
9⅞ x 11⅛ inches
1993.C1384

Taylor's art celebrates the form, texture and pattern of nature. It is robust, viewing nature up close, and reaching out to stroke the trembling leaves stirring in the hot air of distant lowlands. These azaleas are alive, burning bushes of color in a wildly alluring setting.

Anna Taylor approached the terrain of her art as a native. James Calvert Smith, a noted illustrator for various national magazines during the 1940s, painted and drew the Florida landscape through the eyes of an enchanted visitor. His art is a reminder of another element in the art of the South. Southern art is not just about the South, or created by Southerners alone. The full range of art activity in the South encompasses those whose visits, however brief, left behind a document of their temporary presence.

The few drawings and watercolors by Smith which appeared in the former Coggins collection are precise and intriguing. In pencil he renders the palms and desert-like beach stretches of the Florida coast in a familiar chiaroscuro, finished and exact, but devoid of tone and mood. His watercolors are another matter. Watercolor is at once a precise and delicate medium. Smith uses it to great advantage in his blend of flowering branches and flowing water. His colors speak of spring in a refreshing manner, a spring welcomed by one who has known long winters outside the South.

15

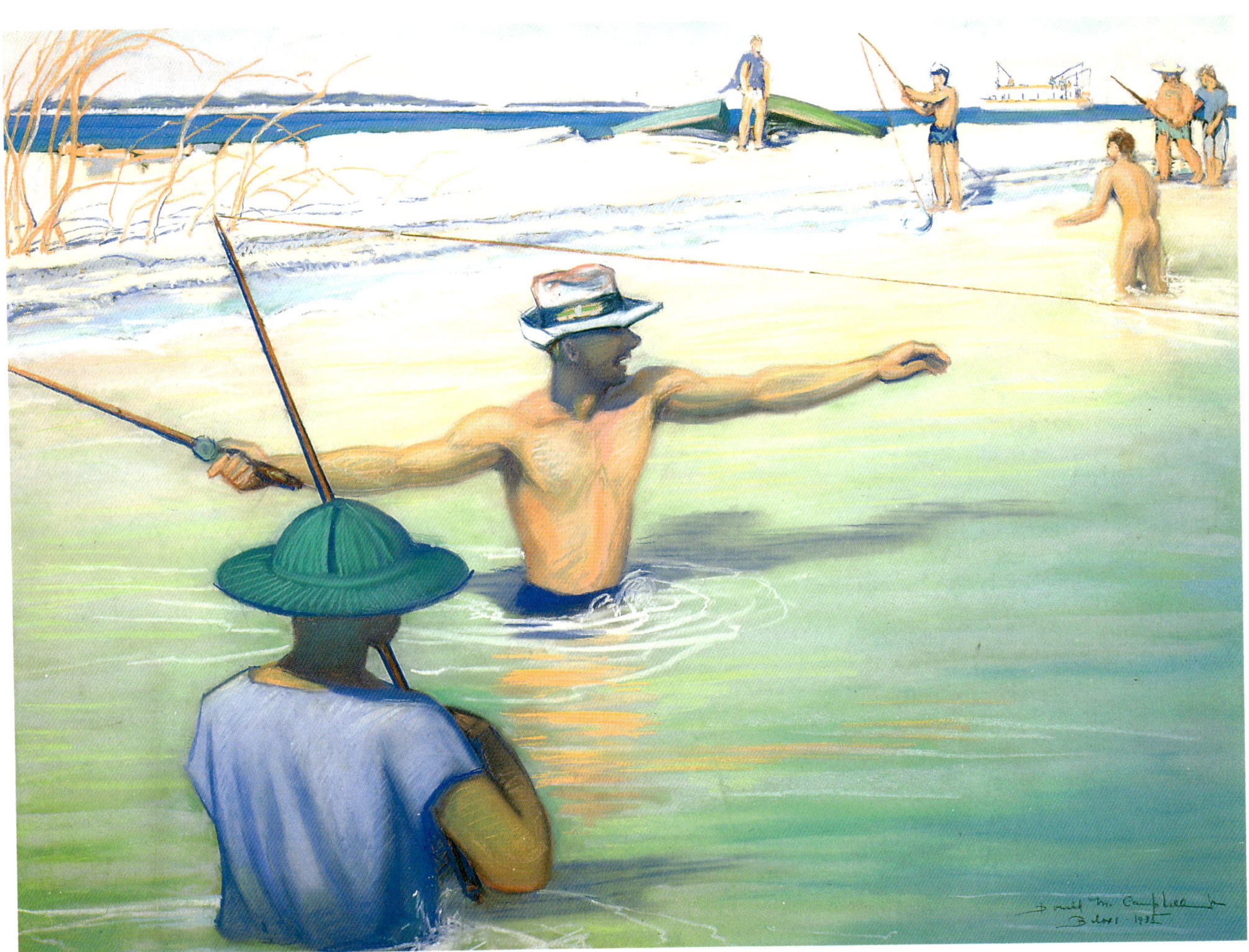

Donald M. Campbell

Surf Fishing

1935

Pastel on paper, 21¾ x 27¾ inches
1992.058

Whether visitor or native, Donald M. Campbell has left behind an intriguing pastel, a work which appears to be a piece of sporting genre – fishermen and bathers out on the beach on a sunny Gulf Coast day. But upon closer examination we can detect a startling transformation. The bather in the upper right hand corner is wandering about totally unclothed in the midst of otherwise bourgeois tourists on the beach. Is he a Depression era nudist, or a subtle footnote of classical intent?

Classicism abounds in other compositional elements. The fisherman whose outstretched arms and smooth musculature dominate the picture plane is not really being caught in a chance cast. His pose is taken directly from the famous fifth century B.C. Greek bronze of Poseidon, discovered off the coast of Eubœa and considered the best preserved extant piece of antiquity.

Nothing is known of Campbell other than this one work. It tells us he had an extensive, and rather clever visual vocabulary. One sporty fisherman in a jaunty straw cap becomes transformed into the God of the Sea, casting his line with a poise and grace that transcends the beach with subliminal erotic power. Behind him the sea and the strolling bathers are mere backdrops for his commanding presence.

These introductory examples suggest the range of ability and the recurrence of certain themes in the works on paper chosen from this collection. At least two of those themes raise issues which have been examined in the past and will persist as subjects of further study. Formula painting, whether of the figure, or the landscape, will continue to blur the line between commercialism and art for art's sake. Consideration of the presentation of the black subject, as well, remains a topic besieged with ambiguity and didactic analysis.

Several very successful Southern artists found a formula which they could practice, often at the risk of being repetitive, to great commercial success. The few surviving drawings by Joseph Rusling Meeker have proven to be topographical dictionaries for his landscape paintings. Solitary birds perched atop lonely pirogues in the bayou appear frequently, as do landscape vistas where a strong foreground draws the viewer into an imaginary depth of ever vaguer detail.

Artists like Elizabeth Verner combine formula with subject matter which tests current interpretative skills. Verner painted the black flower vendors of Charleston almost as often as Meeker painted the swamp. Though skilled, and at times insightful into the characters they portray, their sheer numbers trouble connoisseurs of rarer depictions.

Still, all are part of the history of Southern art activity. Bringing to wider attention the variety of visual expression in the South continues to be the mission of this institution. These works are gathered from a much larger collection which attests to other albums yet to be opened, other landscapes yet to be explored in depth.

— E C P

James Barton Longacre

1794 –1869

Born, Delaware County, Pennsylvania; studied with the engraver George Murray in Philadelphia; active in the South during periodic trips in his capacity as an engraver for the United States Mint, and in the course of establishing his 'The National Portrait Gallery of Distinguished Americans,' especially in Washington and New Orleans; died, Philadelphia.

The Paddle Steamers Homer and General Bryan at the Docks

c. 1838 – 1840

Watercolor on paper, 4¾ x 8¾ inches
1993.C1049

JAMES BARTON LONGACRE WAS ONE OF THE MOST CELEBRATED engravers of the young republic. While still a very young man, he was apprenticed to George Murray, an engraver in Philadelphia, from whom he learned those rudimentary skills which he was to use to much advantage in his later, monumental, documentary activities. In 1819 he went into business for himself, accomplishing a major achievement in 1820 when he engraved the likenesses of the founding fathers on the facsimile of the Declaration of Independence for the Murray concern.

This success brought him to the attention of John Sanderson, whose "Biography of the Signers of the Declaration of Independence" was in progress, and for which Longacre engraved many of the portraits. But these activities were merely a prelude to Longacre's greatest work, the portrait engravings of "The National Portrait Gallery of Distinguished Americans," undertaken with a partner, James Herring. Longacre's goal in publishing the volume was set forth in a high-sounding introduction. Lamenting the absence of "a central repository for the preservation of the Portraits. . . relating to the most distinguished" citizens of the republic, the artists sought to remedy the situation in four monumental octavo volumes.

Once completed, "to a very great extent, the object has been accomplished. The invaluable relics of those whose lives have most eminently contributed to the formation of our character and proud distinction as a self-governed people have in many instances been saved from destruction or wrested from oblivion."

Small works by Longacre, such as *The Paddle Steamers Homer and General Bryan at the Docks*, are quite rare. After 1844, he became an engraver for the United States Mint in Philadelphia, and his personal artistic output declined. This work is clearly related to a trip to New Orleans thought to have been undertaken by the artist in 1840. Conversations held with Robert G. Stewart, Chief Curator of the National Portrait Gallery, and the artist's principal biographer, indicate that such a trip was made, perhaps for business purposes. The unmistakable profile of the city, facing the crescent of the river, with the boats docked in the vicinity of Governor Nichols and Barracks Streets is visible in the background.

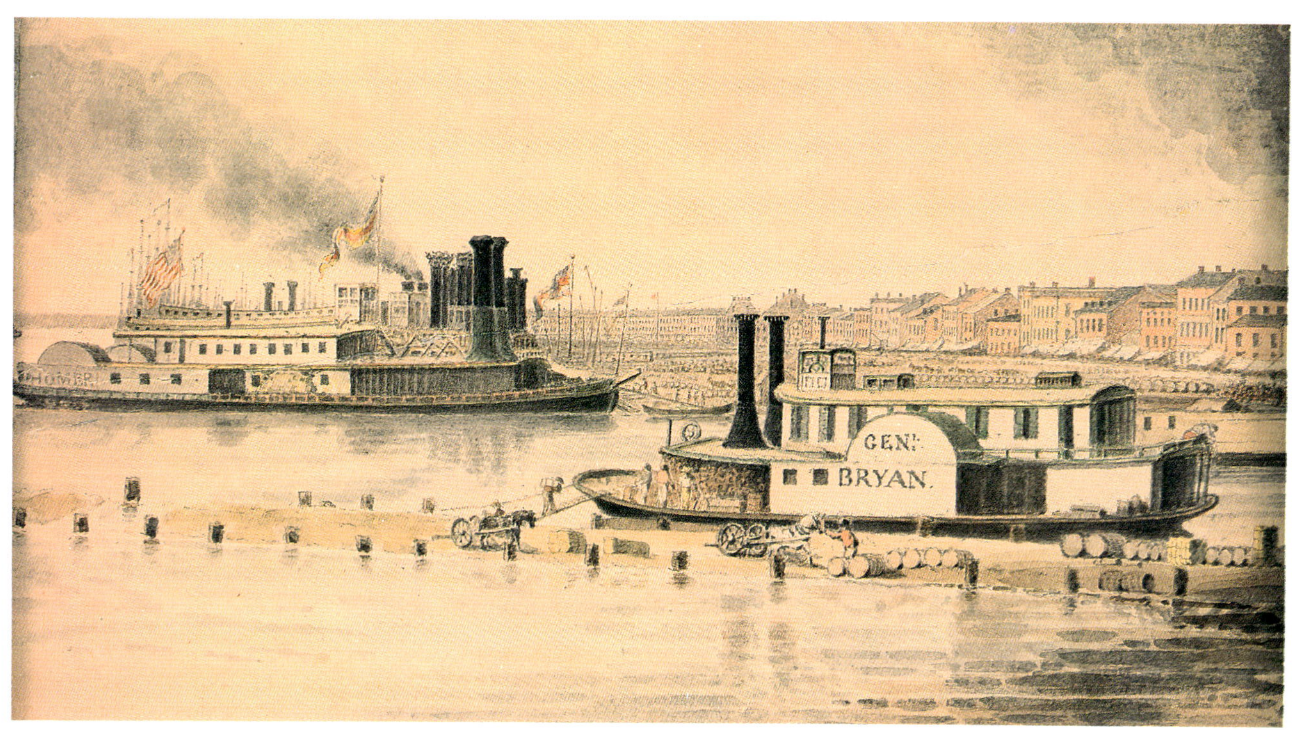

George Washington Sully

1816 – 1890

Born, Norfolk, Virginia; no formal training, but as the nephew of the artists Robert Matthew Sully and Thomas Sully, received considerable studio exposure; active in North Florida, at Magnolia, Appalachicola, Aspalaga, Tallahassee and St. Mark's, 1833-1839; in Virginia in 1840, and thereafter in New Orleans; died, Covington, Louisiana.

New Orleans Rack Picture

c. 1840

Watercolor on paper, 6½ x 8 inches
1989.01.100

GEORGE WASHINGTON SULLY WAS A NEPHEW OF THE CELEBRATED painter Thomas Sully. His father, Chester Sully, was the subject of one of Thomas Sully's first forays into the style of romantic portraiture he established as a national benchmark. Whether Sully received any instruction from his famous uncle is uncertain; at any rate, the family moved to the Florida west coast in the early 1820s.

Young Sully's first artistic efforts were rather flat landscape views of Florida, and sketches of a trip to Bermuda. While charming, these are of greater antiquarian interest as records of settlement and architecture than for any lasting proof they give of greater ability. Most of these were rendered prior to 1834 when the artist was still a youth. After his father's death in 1834 the family moved to New Orleans, where G. W. Sully eventually became a successful cotton broker.

The still-life "rack picture" at hand is rather unusual. While the rack painting format would become an established style in late nineteenth century American still-life art, it would seldom have been seen in antebellum New Orleans, save perhaps in printed form. Derived from certain seventeenth century art forms, notably the *vanitas* tradition of Dutch still-life painting in the golden age, it is an art form in which one searches, or even flounders after mysterious embedded meaning.

Prior to the rise of widespread visual imagery in mass produced form, the printed or drawn word and image had a totemic power suggestive of identity and function. A "Protestant merchant society" according to John Wilmerding in his work on John F. Peto and American still-life painting, "like that (of nineteenth-century America) valued the practical, the orderly, and the immediate. It follows that its art would include images of currency, and familiar objects from the domestic environment."

Whatever its meaning, Sully has given us an entree into a merchant society, which if not altogether Protestant, surely seethed with the same fertile multi-cultural cross-fertilization found in any prosperous port, be it Amsterdam, or New Orleans. Sully's rack suspends reminders of the interaction between New York and New Orleans as major points of exchange. The agricultural produce of the lower Mississippi made the journey north, even as New Orleans received goods, in the obscured personage hidden behind the ribbon, whose function as a "commission merchant" is clearly visible.

It is tempting to think that we do not know the entire story Sully tells. Is this a mere random assemblage of business cards and commodity menus, or the oblique biography of a vanished class of mercantile pioneers supplying a culture poised between frontier and civilization?

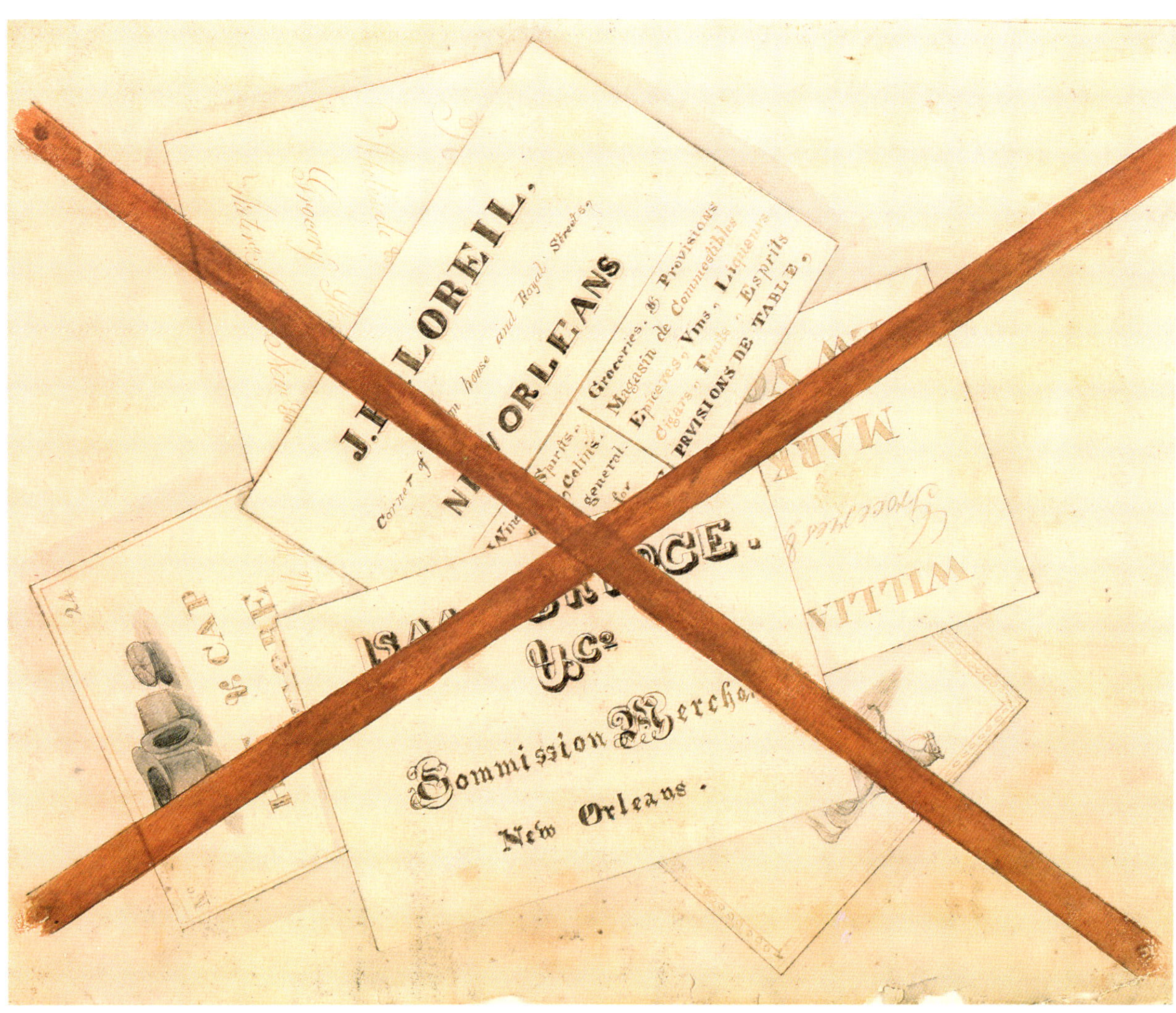

Joseph Rusling Meeker

1827–1889

*Born, Newark, New Jersey; studied at the National
Academy of Design, 1845; active in Louisville,
Kentucky, 1852-1859, and in Louisiana, 1861-1865;
thought to have made intermittent sketching trips to
the Mississippi Delta area, 1865-1875; died,
St. Louis.*

A Louisiana Swamp

c. 1870

Charcoal and white chalk on paper, 15⅝ x 19 inches
1989.01.116

DURING MEEKER'S TENURE AS A PAYMASTER ON A UNION GUNBOAT
patrolling the backwaters of the upper Mississippi delta in the late
years of the Civil War, he is thought to have collected visual ideas
and images that resulted in the great landscape art he created
between 1865 and 1878. Whether he brought back actual sketches
from his wartime sojourn, upon which he based subsequent paintings,
or drew those sketches on later trips, is a mystery perpetuated by
this particular drawing.

Louisiana Bayou, now in the Ogden Collection, is Meeker's
earliest painting deploying those vocabularial forms drawn from his
sketches, and typifies his approach to the murky landscape through
which he sailed. The strong foreground, behind which the evocatively
moist rear ground stands as a vaporous foil for the assorted
naturalistic elements defining the setting, are all rendered with a
subtle palette, tonalist in lingering romantic coloration, proto-tonalist
in the slight color variations which emphasize the evasive, distant
quality of the actual scene.

Although none of these painterly effects are as apparent in the
sketches, they do define the artist's vocabulary. While Meeker was
quite specific about laying down color, adjusting "major and minor"
lights, he was just as specific about the elements in his landscapes.
Here we see the solitary bird poised attentively on the prow of the
pirogue, the tall, tapering trees creating a naturalistic proscenium
arch, and the trailing moss and vine embellishing the wilderness
wonderland.

Meeker's quest for these scenes is vaguely documented by one
brief newspaper account noting he left St. Louis "occasionally during
the summer months to get material for new pictures." This drawing
tells us much of what that material consisted, and so it is at once a
charming late nineteenth century drawing and a rare art historical
document.

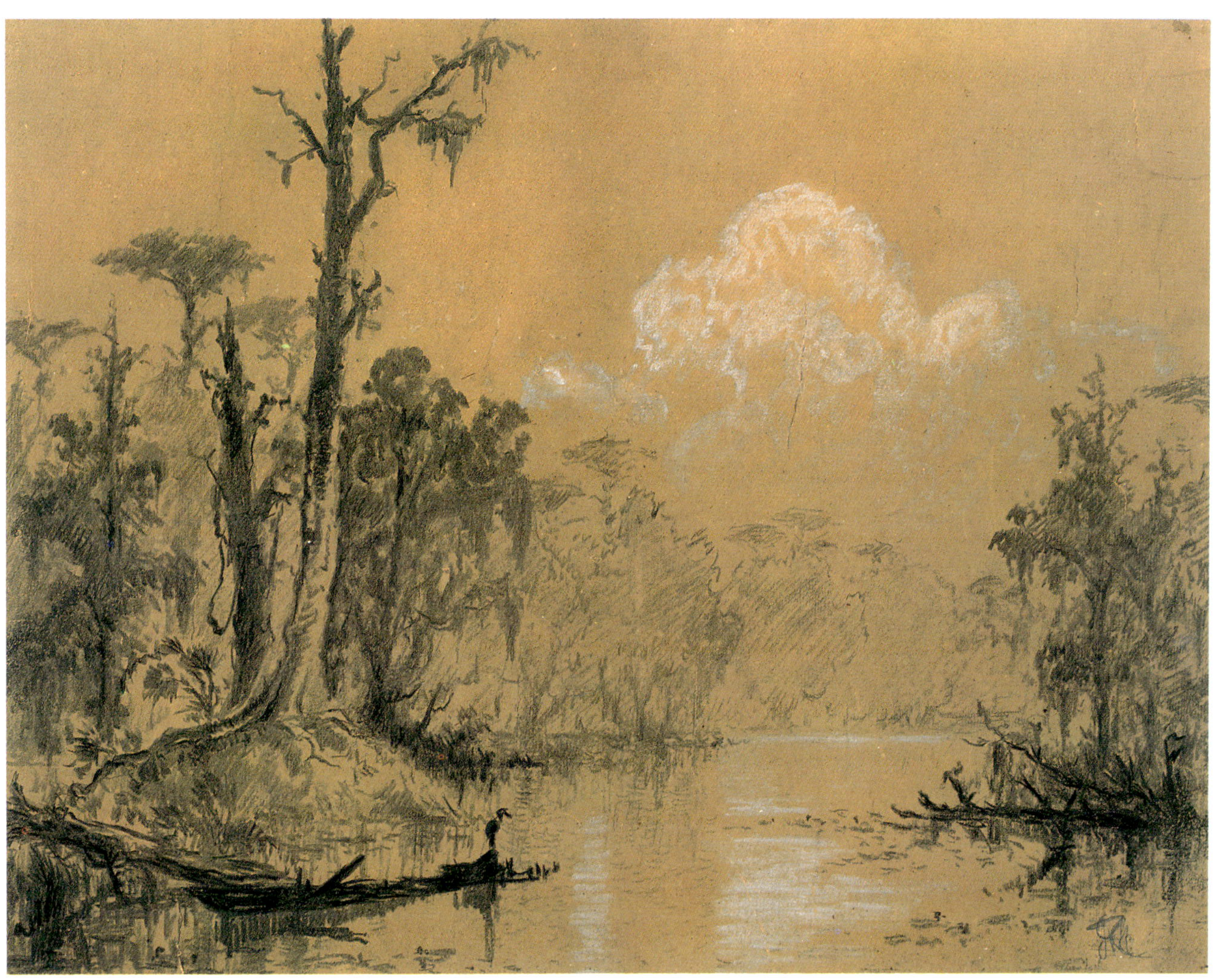

John Ross Key

1832 – 1920

Born, Hagerstown, Maryland; studied in Munich, Paris, and at the National Academy of Design, 1856-1857; active in the South at Charleston, 1863, and in Baltimore throughout his life; died, Baltimore.

Landscape

1876

Mixed media on paper, 11⅛ x 19⅛ inches
1993.C0379

AS THE GRANDSON OF THE AUTHOR OF THE LYRICS TO "THE STAR Spangled Banner," Key's support of the Confederate cause during the Civil War was ironic, but typical of the divided loyalties which color that tragic event. A lieutenant in the Confederate Engineers, he was stationed at Fort Sumter from 1863 until 1865. During that time he painted the remarkable panoramic view of the bombardment which is now in the collection of the Greenville County Museum of Art in South Carolina.

Following the war, Key continued his artistic career, painting and drawing in the upper South, especially in Virginia and along the Eastern Shore. When he exhibited a group of charcoal drawings in Boston in 1877 they were praised as "among the best ever shown here in Boston, firm and masterly, strong and graceful."

As has been noted by at least one scholar, Key's mastery of depth and perspective is considerably enhanced by his formal understanding of the horizontal possibilities of the picture plane.

In the great bombardment painting he brings the full panoramic sweep of Charleston harbor into sight. Here, he juxtaposes the line of the water's edge with the figures in the foreground and the looming mountain behind, all drawn with a very solid sense of mass, rendered in a rich, deep hue, to create a work of engaging presence, resonant with chiaroscuro atmospherics while at the same time projecting the stark values of contemporary photographic imagery.

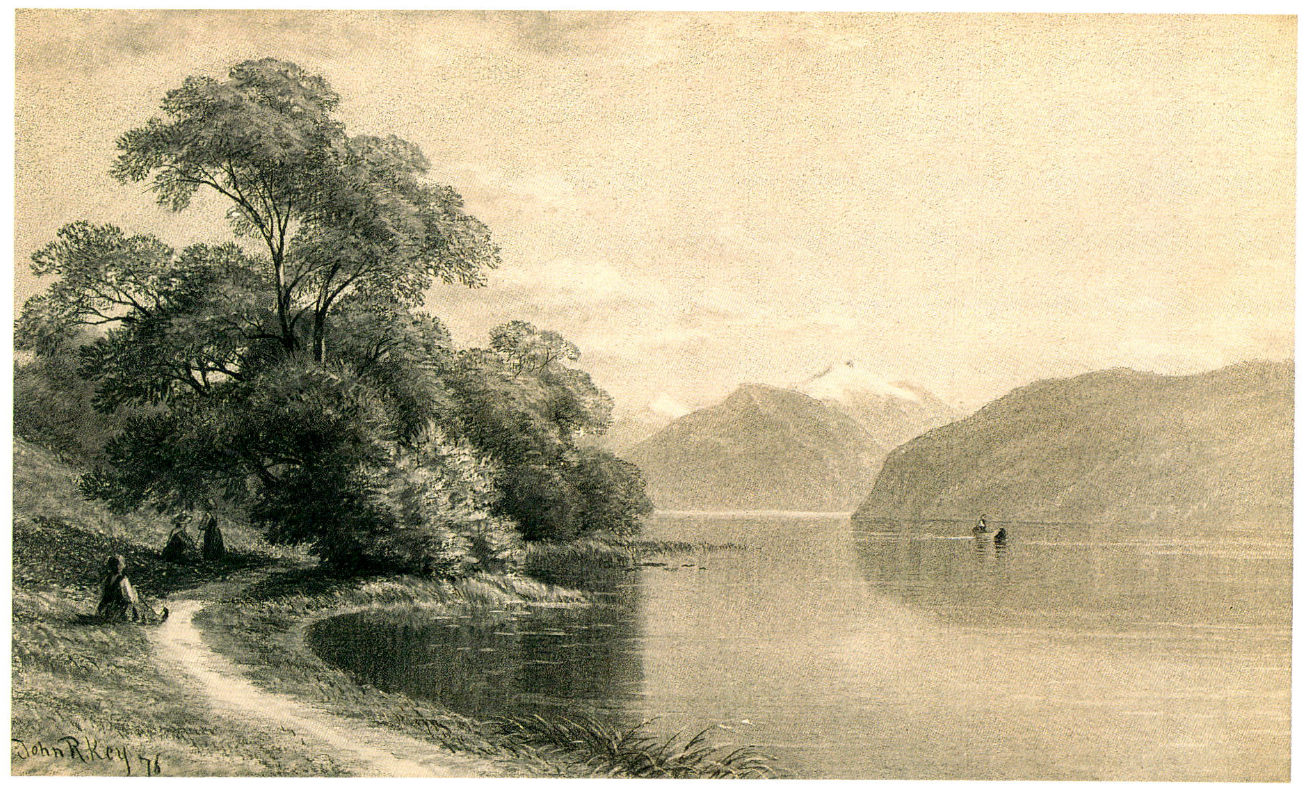

Robert Burns Wilson

1850/1? – 1916

Born, Washington County, Pennsylvania; studied in Pittsburgh, with John White Alexander, 1871; active in Kentucky, at Lexington, Frankfort, and Louisville, 1871-1904; died, New York City(?).

Lions

c. 1890

Pastel on paper, 14 ½ x 21 inches
1990.019

ROBERT BURNS WILSON SHOULD ENGAGE OUR ATTENTION, IF FOR no other reason than the fact that he travelled to Union County, Kentucky from Pittsburgh in 1871 by canoe, surely a rather prodigious feat. Once in Kentucky, he did set about to paint in a uniquely personal style, mostly formulaic landscapes extolling the beauties of the Central Kentucky plateau, in moody tonalist shades. He also painted, in watercolor, several tightly-drawn, full-length portraits of Frankfort natives, including the children of Orlando Brown, all in a charmingly reduced scale.

Wilson had decided literary ambitions as well. Between about 1875 and his death in 1915, he published three small volumes of poems and a novel, *Until The Day Break*. Most of these poems were rather prosaic affairs, celebrating the struggle between human will and the superior forces of nature, which always subdue our instincts and bend our feeble desires to the natural cyclic flow of life.

This rather large, and certainly well-developed watercolor marks a genuine departure for Wilson. Whereas his formulaic landscape works have been seen as decidedly sentimental, showing a fondness of blue shadings and hazes that conceal rugged and unpleasant details, this is a work of subtle symbolist authority. Like the Orientalists, particularly Jean Leon Gerome, Wilson appropriates the lion as a symbol of the power of savage nature, in harmony with the world he dominates, and over which he, like the glowing passage of light, presides with a will free from the constraints of articulate human concern.

Ironically enough, in his own lifetime Wilson was known as the man who penned the poem "Remember The Maine," which became the battle cry of the Spanish-American War.

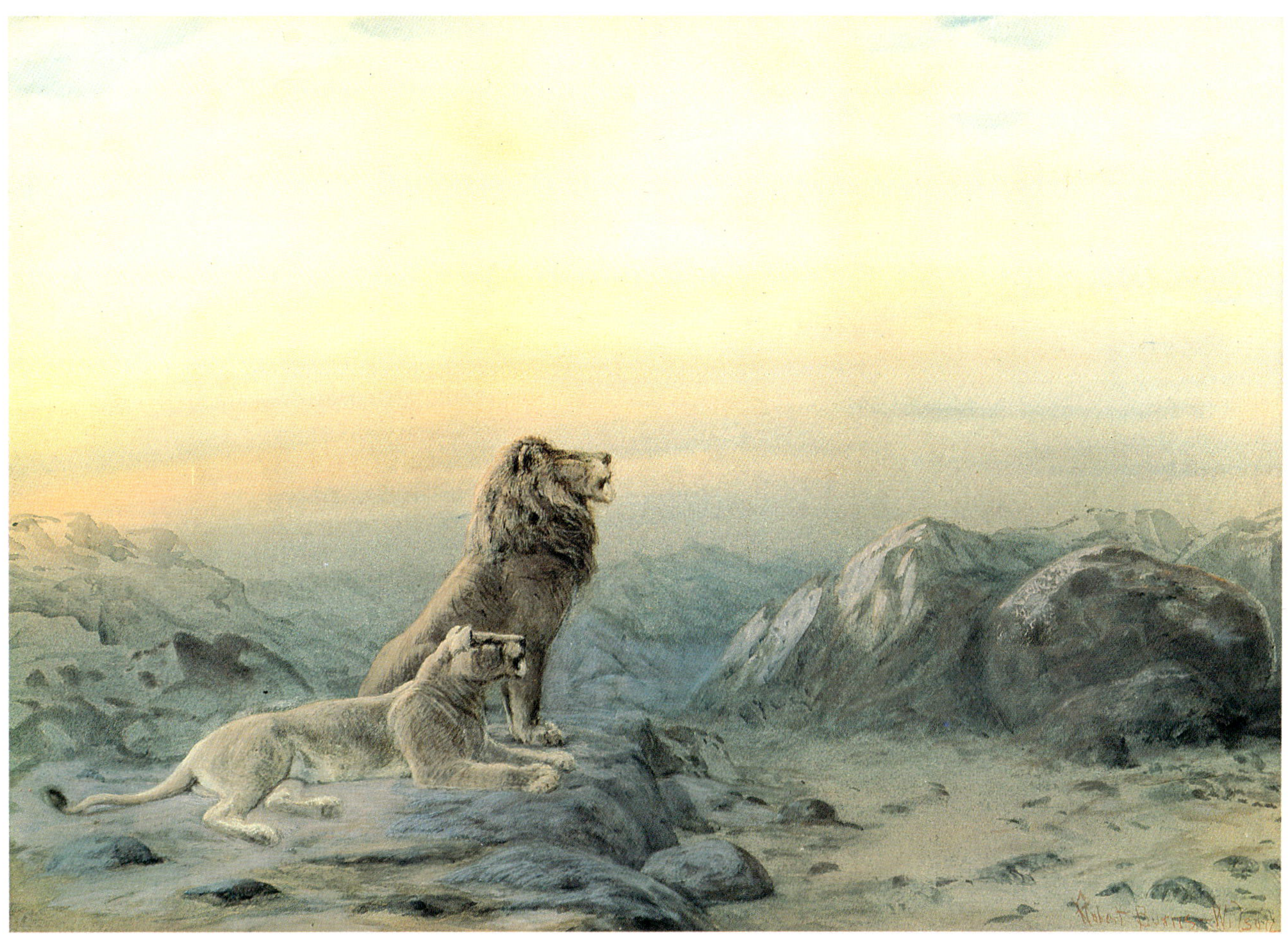

Ellsworth Woodward

1861–1939

*Born, Seekonk, Massachusetts; studied, Rhode Island
School of Design, 1878-1880, and in Munich,
Germany, 1884; active in New Orleans, 1885-1939;
died, New Orleans.*

Bayou St. John Waterway

c. 1910

Watercolor on paper, 14⅜ x 19 inches
1992.007

DURING HIS LONG CAREER AS A PAINTER, TEACHER, AND ART
administrator, Ellsworth Woodward fulfilled a mission in creating
a viable climate for art expression under the auspices of Newcomb
College, Tulane University, and at the Delgado Museum in New
Orleans. Woodward was the product of a very fine academic
tradition, first at the Rhode Island School of Design and subsequently
in Munich where, like William Merritt Chase, he seems to have
absorbed the brilliant technique of light/dark contrasts which
epitomizes the Germanic synthesis of Old Master painterliness with
Impressionist coloration.

Fortunately, Woodward left behind a large body of writing,
which clarifies his aesthetic. Although deeply conservative both in
training and in his insistence on certain academic standards,
Woodward saw himself as a progressive pioneer, attempting to
reform Southern art expression. In that area he saw "a lessening
volume of traditional, sentimental, and tritely objective painting, and
a growing volume of adventurous struggle toward the expression of
ideas and the interpretation of nature and art."

Woodward was a superb watercolorist. Fluid, richly colored, and
very subtly balanced, his works evoke the watery world of the
swamps and bayous around the city whose shining surfaces bounced
back brilliant tropical light. In the New Orleans area Woodward
found a place with "personality and charm which exerts a spell over
sensitive souls yielding themselves to its influence. Technique was a
matter of balancing observation and inspiration. "We have before us
a landscape. How will you go about reducing it to a painted picture?
Everything your eye rests upon has equal value. If you are to imitate
these things, you are defeated before you begin. No, if we are to
produce a work of art, we must select, arrange, eliminate, simplify
and bend all we see to what we feel. . . ."

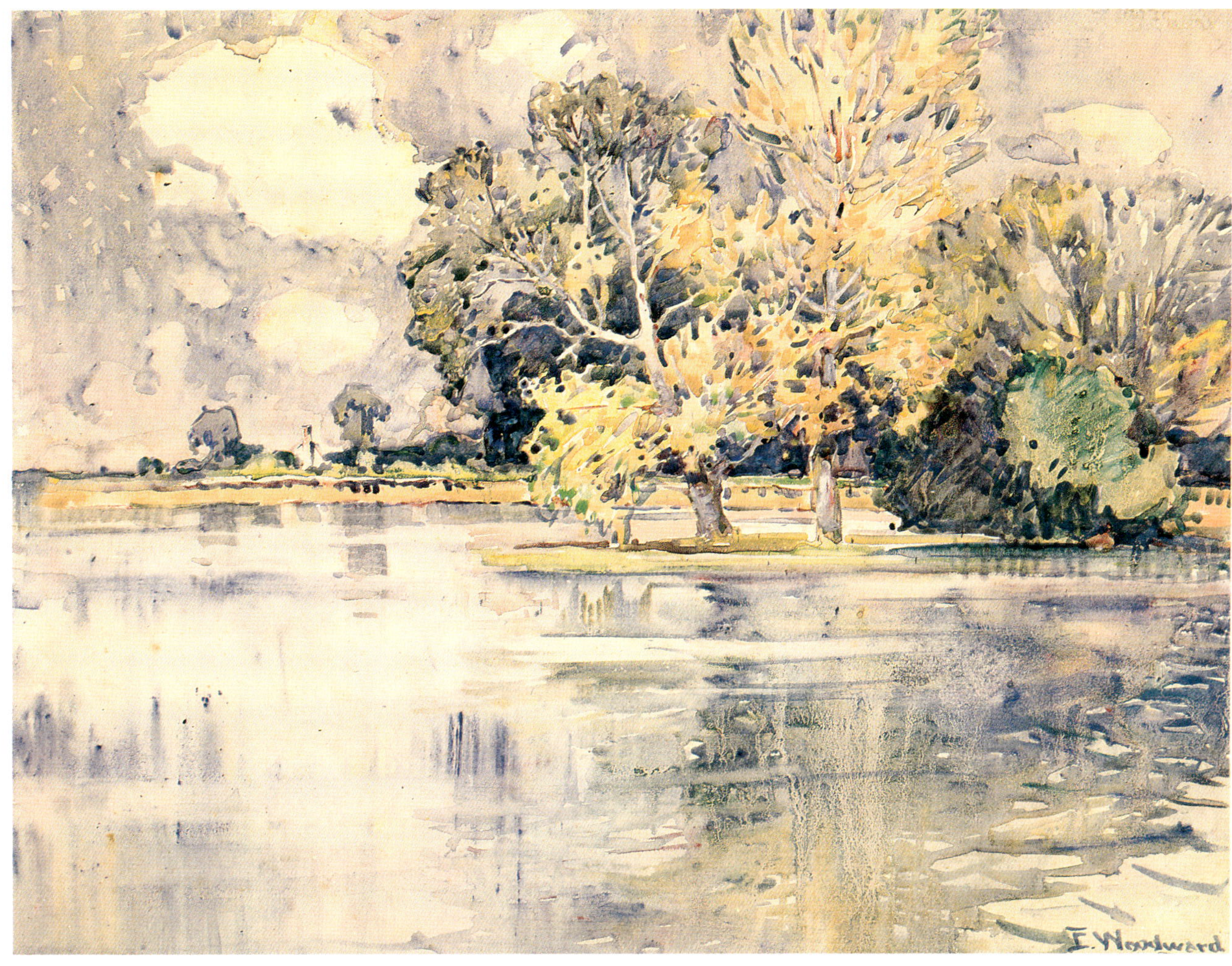
F. Woodward

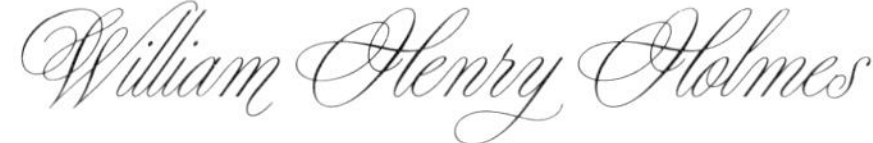

William Henry Holmes

1846 – 1933

Born near Cadiz, Ohio; studied at the Willoughby Collegiate Institute in Cleveland, Ohio, 1870, and with Theodore Kauffmann in Washington, D.C., 1871-1872, and with Frank Duveneck in Munich, 1879; active in the Washington, D.C. area throughout his artistic career; died, Royal Oak, Michigan.

Girl Sitting on a Hillside

c.1910

Watercolor on paper, 14¼ x 21 inches
1992.053

ALTHOUGH WILLIAM HENRY HOLMES EVENTUALLY RECEIVED FORMAL training in art, he was largely self-taught. For that matter he was largely self-taught in all the academic disciplines in which he excelled, until he came to the attention of the Smithsonian Institution through his own efforts. Like some character in a Victorian morality play, he endeavored, with the result that the "mobility evident in his career indicates that he used his talents to make the most of every opportunity for advancement," according to Clifford M. Nelson.

His first advances resulted from ingratiating himself with the organizers of several Smithsonian geological survey teams exploring the west in the 1870s. Upon his return, he produced several panoramas and sections of panoramas which were highly acclaimed then, and continue to be well regarded as topographical art. Thereafter he worked his way through the Smithsonian bureaucracy to become an art director and natural history administrator of considerable prestige and authority.

Though a practicing artist during a period of great change, Holmes expressed little esteem for revolutionary movements, often referring to the "lunacy of impressionism." He did exhibit with several Washington art clubs, painting and continuing to develop as an artist right up until the time of his final illness.

Despite his protestations, Holmes' best works are truly in the impressionist idiom. While his oils have a certain Ruskinian air of truth in their depiction of nature, his watercolors are about light and air and space. Many of those which survive in Smithsonian collections depict the area around the District of Columbia, at that time a rather small town with easy access to country roads and fields.

Girl Sitting on a Hillside balances the clever compositional device of organizing the picture plane on an angle prompted by the slant of the hill, and using a subtle palette. Punctuating his close color harmonics with bravura splashes of color and brushstroke, Holmes achieves that most cherished impressionist aim: to dissolve the harsh edges of the scene in a blur of enticing color and light.

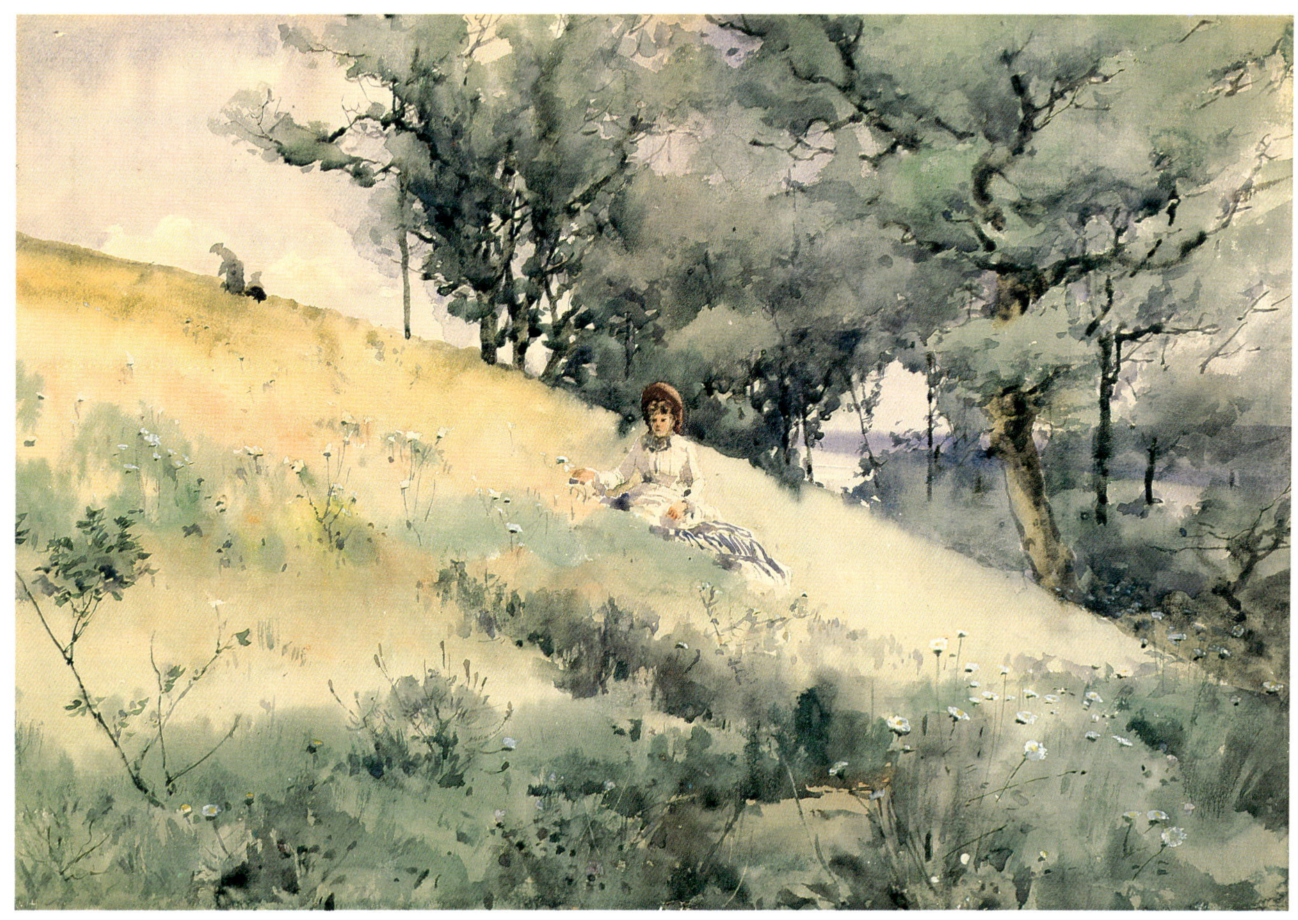

Charles Ephraim Burchfield

1893 – 1967

*Born, Ashtabula Harbor, Ohio; studied at the
Cleveland School of Art with Henry Keller and
Frank Wilcox, 1911-1916; active in the South,
while on duty at Camp Jackson, South Carolina,
1918; died, New York City.*

Early Night

1918

Graphite on paper, 8¼ x 5 inches
1989.01.023

IN 1918 THE FLEDGLING ARTIST CHARLES BURCHFIELD WAS CALLED up for duty in World War I and posted to Camp Jackson, South Carolina. To that point Burchfield's struggles to become an artist had been confined mostly to his efforts in a wallpaper factory. Already he was showing those strains of melancholy, fantastic, fluid composition and visionary naturalism which distinguish his work. While on duty in South Carolina he kept a small sketchbook in which he recorded camp life and the local scene. John I. H. Baur, his biographer, finds that most of these drawings "have a sad and haunted look. . . ." Burchfield himself, in his unpublished diary, speaks of being "lost in Negro Fairyland," perhaps indicating that he found the power and mystery of local black folklife as inspiring as had several generations of his fellow artists. In 1930 one of his drawings became a large watercolor *Souvenir of South Carolina* which shows a group of blacks before a country store chatting and visiting beneath unusually calm tree limbs.

As with Walter Anderson, much has been made of Burchfield's writhing, undulating, naturalist forms and his propensity to invest nature with an awesome, unseen power. Like Anderson, his fierce devotion to portraying the inner life of the outer world was nourished – and guarded – in relative seclusion.

Implicit qualities within Burchfield's work always seem poised to overwhelm those without. His art is another example of artistic celebration of nature as a vehicle for expressing the lurking threat of the world around us, rather than as sunny days spent wandering in wondrous woods. Though small and vaguely detailed, *Early Night* contains much of the spirit of Burchfield's later works. In sharp profile, flimsy camp tents sit awkwardly before a wood which yawns and gapes behind them. Through the trees we see a dark and penetrating space beneath the limbs which rise and join like bombed out cathedral windows, beckoning us to look into a distant void which swallows up all light and allows no further glimpse of what lies beyond.

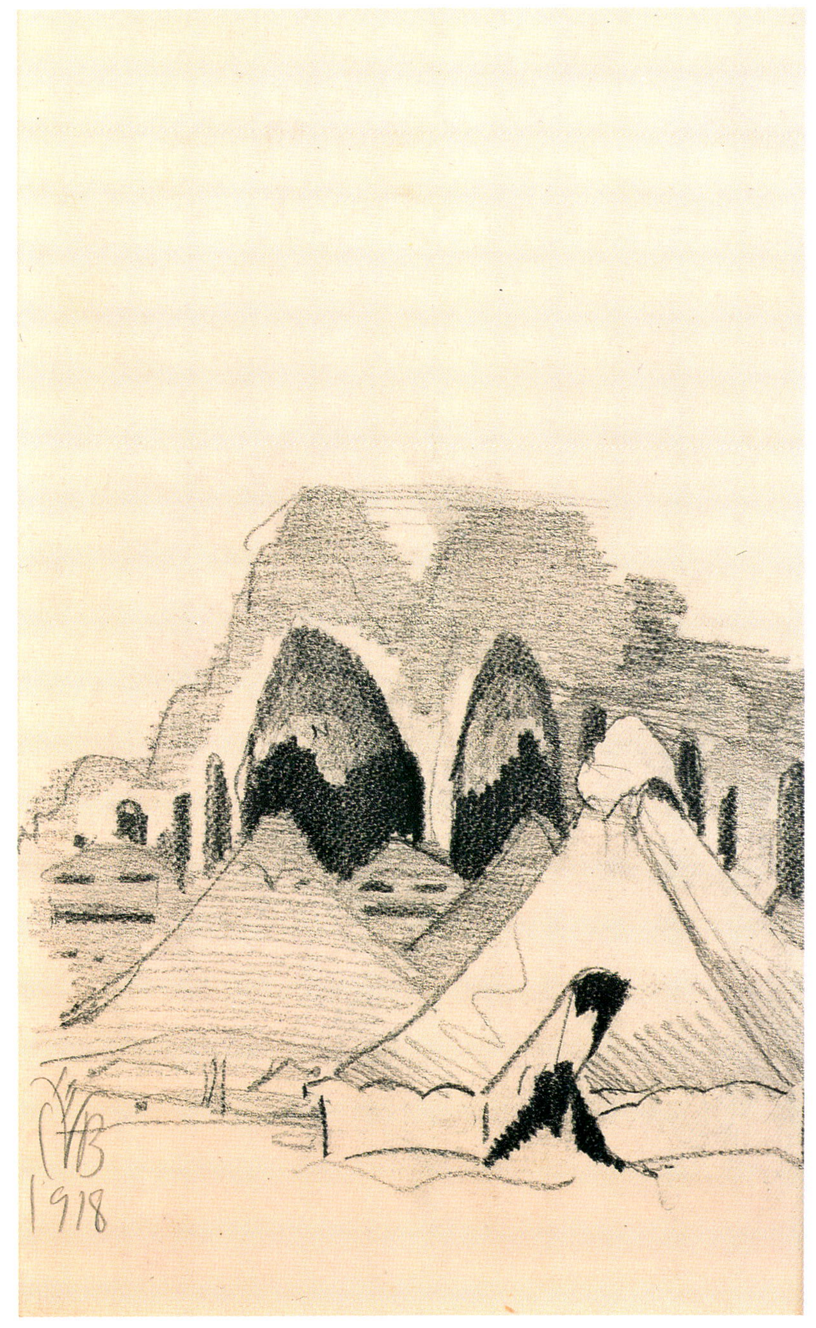

William Robinson Leigh

1866 – 1955?

Born, Berkeley County, West Virginia; studied at the Maryland Institute, Baltimore, with Hugh Newell 1880-1883, and at the Munich Academy; active in the South in West Virginia, at intermittent periods throughout his career; died, New York(?).

Maidstone Manor

1918

Mixed media on paper, 18 ⅞ x 13 ⅞ inches
1993.C1437

WILLIAM ROBINSON LEIGH WAS BORN IN A STATELY OLD VIRGINIA home to circumstances which typified the genteel Southern spirit of the day. Though Southern by birth, Leigh harbored a childhood ambition to travel to the West and chronicle the life and times of the frontier. To achieve that dream, Leigh received highly traditional academic training both in this country and in France. Accordingly, his work has that same spirit of fantastic realism (seen in the attention to detail) and the panoramic compositional sweep that can be seen in the history and genre paintings of Edwin Austin Abbey and William Alphonse Bougereau.

Leigh made numerous trips to the West, and to Africa as well, but this drawing gives proof that he returned on at least one contemplative occasion to the place of his birth. Maidstone Manor, where he was born, was built in 1848 in Falling Waters, in what is now West Virginia. The square mass of the house itself, a familiar four up/four down room plan, divided by a central hall, is relieved by the graceful proportions of the Greek Revival portico shading the wide sidelit doorway.

Leigh's delicate drawing, capturing the house at an inviting angle, has the look and feel of a frontispiece for a book by one of his fellow Virginians, Thomas Nelson Page. While the white chalk atmosphere on sepia ground conveys just the right strain of nostalgia, the drawing is also a visual footnote, a quiet reminder of this Western artist's Southern past.

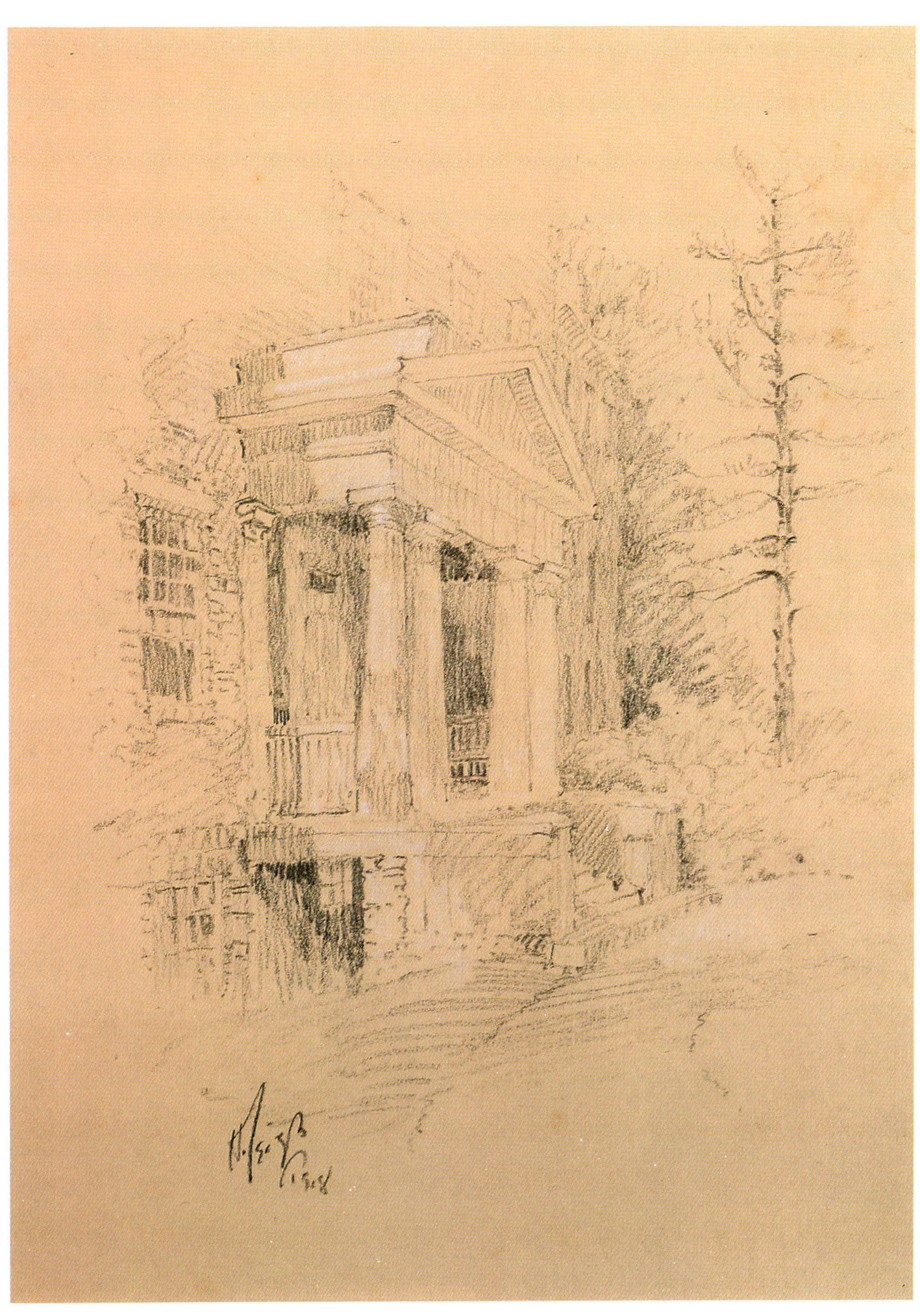

*Alice Ravenel
Huger Smith*

1876 – 1958

*Born and died Charleston, South Carolina, where
she was active as an artist throughout her life.*

Waterway in Springtime

c. 1915

Watercolor on paper, 12½ x 6½ inches
1993.C8004

ALICE SMITH'S SCANT TRAINING INCLUDED TAKING CLASSES, WHEN very young, from Mlle. L.L. Fery at the Carolina Art Association in Charleston. From this French instructor she was exposed to certain impressionist ideas, notably, reports Martha Severens, "the rule that watercolor should always be transparent and never to use opaque color." She also appealed to Birge Harrison for critique and instruction on his trip to Charleston in 1910, but his tonalist works in the Barbizon mood seem to have had little impact upon her.

It was her fascination with the delicacy of Japanese art that was to become most apparent in her evanescent watercolor style. Attracted to both prints and watercolors, she tried her hand at a variety of media, finally settling down, around 1924, to a long pursuit of watercolors. Her organization of the planar space, which avoids suggestive three-dimensionality, affirms her ongoing interest in both the spirituality and techniques of the Oriental way.

Severens has described how Smith "laid her paper flat on a table, (and) stood above it and brushed on her colors. She rarely wiped them off, allowing for surprisingly fluid, yet brilliant tones." This technique was often applied to her memory sketches, where she attempted to capture "the essence of the landscape and its mood, rather than the structure and detail of it."

Though comparatively small, the previously unpublished watercolor in this collection has precisely those qualities most admired in the artist's work. The fluid overlaying of colors blends toward a central point of light bursting through the foliage in a spot of yellow fire subdued by the dense atmospheric moisture. Impressionistic in mood, it is also spontaneous and immediate, a pensive moment in a remote wood, enlivened by a deeply personal sense of color and light.

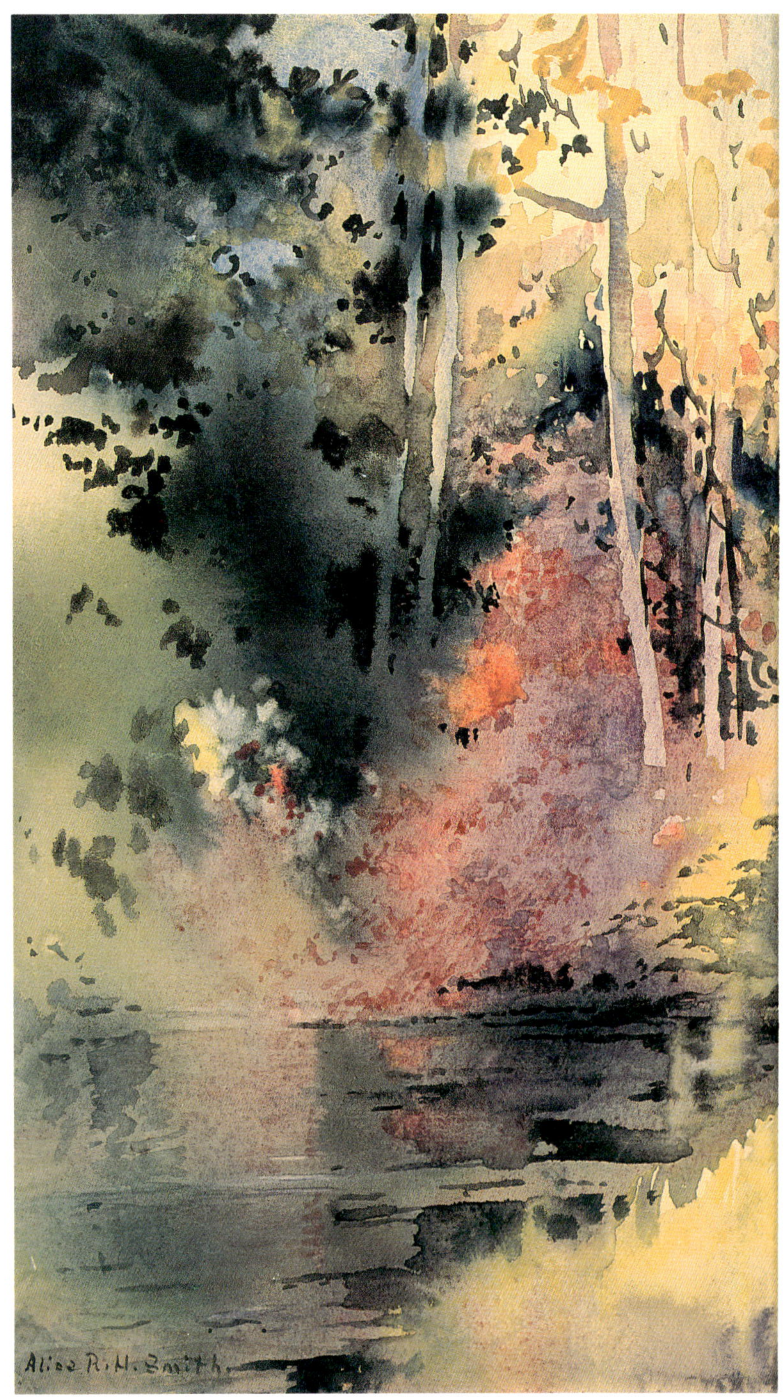
Alice R.H. Smith

*Sarah Agnes
Estelle Irvine*

1887 – 1970

*Born, New Orleans; studied at Newcomb College of
Tulane University, New Orleans, with the Woodward
brothers, and at the Art Students League, New York,
c.1906; active in New Orleans throughout her career;
died, New Orleans.*

Young Man with a Violin

c. 1915

Pastel on paper, 10½ x 8½ inches
1990.090

SADIE IRVINE WAS BEST KNOWN AS ONE OF SEVERAL HIGHLY
prolific decorators for the Newcomb Pottery wares produced in the
golden age of that group, 1906-1936. She had been trained by
Ellsworth Woodward, as can be seen in her signature coloration,
format of her watercolors and the blue/green of her "moss and
moon" pottery designs.

Miss Irvine also studied, at least briefly, at the Art Students
League in New York. It is in her drawings that we see the best
evidence of her New York experience. The Art Students League at
that period was a center for drawing from life, and was one of the
most important centers for formal training in America. Under the
direction of such master teachers as Frank Vincent Dumond and
Robert Reid, several generations of young Southern women learned
to draw and perfected those native talents which they may have
already developed in genteel amateur circumstances in the South.

Young Man With a Violin has all the direct power and immediacy
that a delicate line drawing can convey. Sadie Irvine's drawings, like
her pottery designs, have a deceptive simplicity of form, a quiet line
in design that neither suggests formal depth and perspective nor
descends to mere caricature. As we look we might be waiting, at a
discreet distance, for the music to begin.

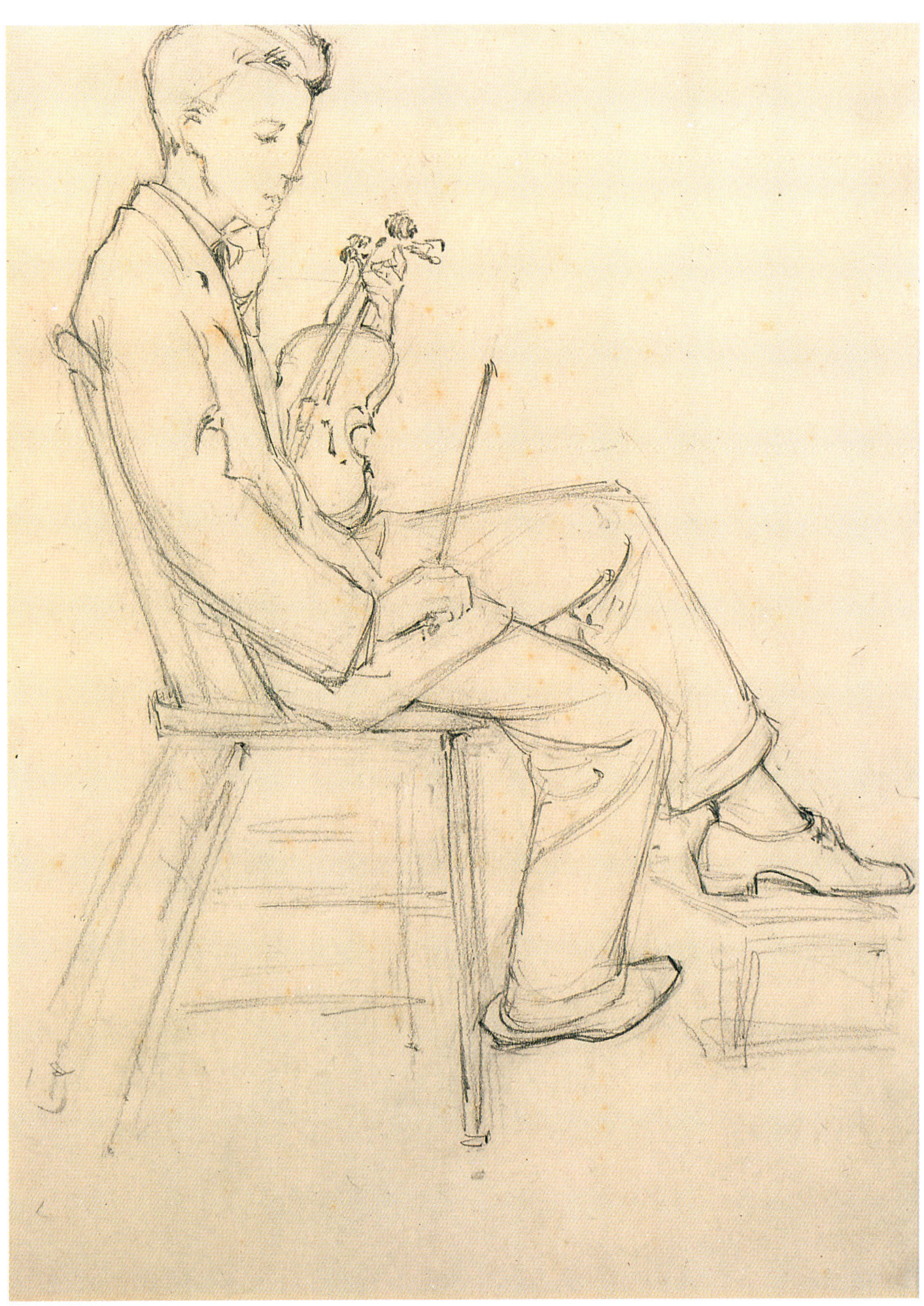

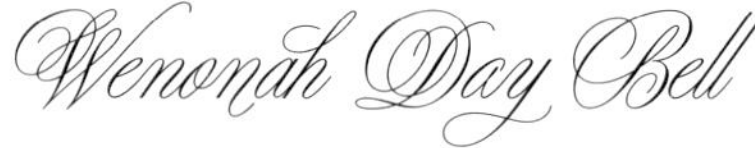

1889 – 1981

Born, Trenton, South Carolina; studied at Brenau College, Gainesville, Georgia, 1908-1910, at the University of Pennsylvania, 1910-1912, and subsequently at the Colarossi Academy in Paris, France, the Hans Hofmann School in Munich and Capri, Columbia Teachers College in New York City, and at the Pennsylvania Academy of Fine Art, 1921-1926; active in Georgia, from her family's base in Greenville, Georgia, throughout her career; died, Greenville.

Greenville, Georgia

1921

Watercolor on paper, 17¼ x 24 inches
1989.01.012

FROM HER MODEST SOUTHERN BACKGROUND, WHICH INCLUDED THE best art training available at Breneau College in Gainesville, Georgia, Wenonah Bell went on to some of the most prestigious art academies in the world. Having studied in Pennsylvania and in Paris, she returned to Philadelphia in 1921, staying until 1926. During that time the excellence of her work earned her the Cresson Award, which allowed her to travel to Europe during the summers for further exposure to trends in contemporary art.

From a Southern standpoint, it is interesting to note that her stay at the P. A. F. A. coincided with those of Walter Anderson and Hugh Breckenridge. While the more extreme elements of contemporary art were not *au courant* in those environs, a spirit of minimal line in design persisted. Anderson's art suggests that the principles of Jay Hambidge, as set forth in his work, "Dynamic Symmetry," were an expressive part of the climate of style.

This may account for the flat, simplified forms of Bell's art. Her more notable paintings have a proto-analytic-cubist flair, flattening figural elements in the foreground against a densely patterned rear ground painted in highly keyed colors.

Watercolor, it has often been noted, was Bell's favorite medium. In works like this domestic view of Greenville, her bold colors seem to enclose the vast white spaces of architecture and terrain into a quietly ordered setting whose similar color values render an intimate view with a deceptively modernist air.

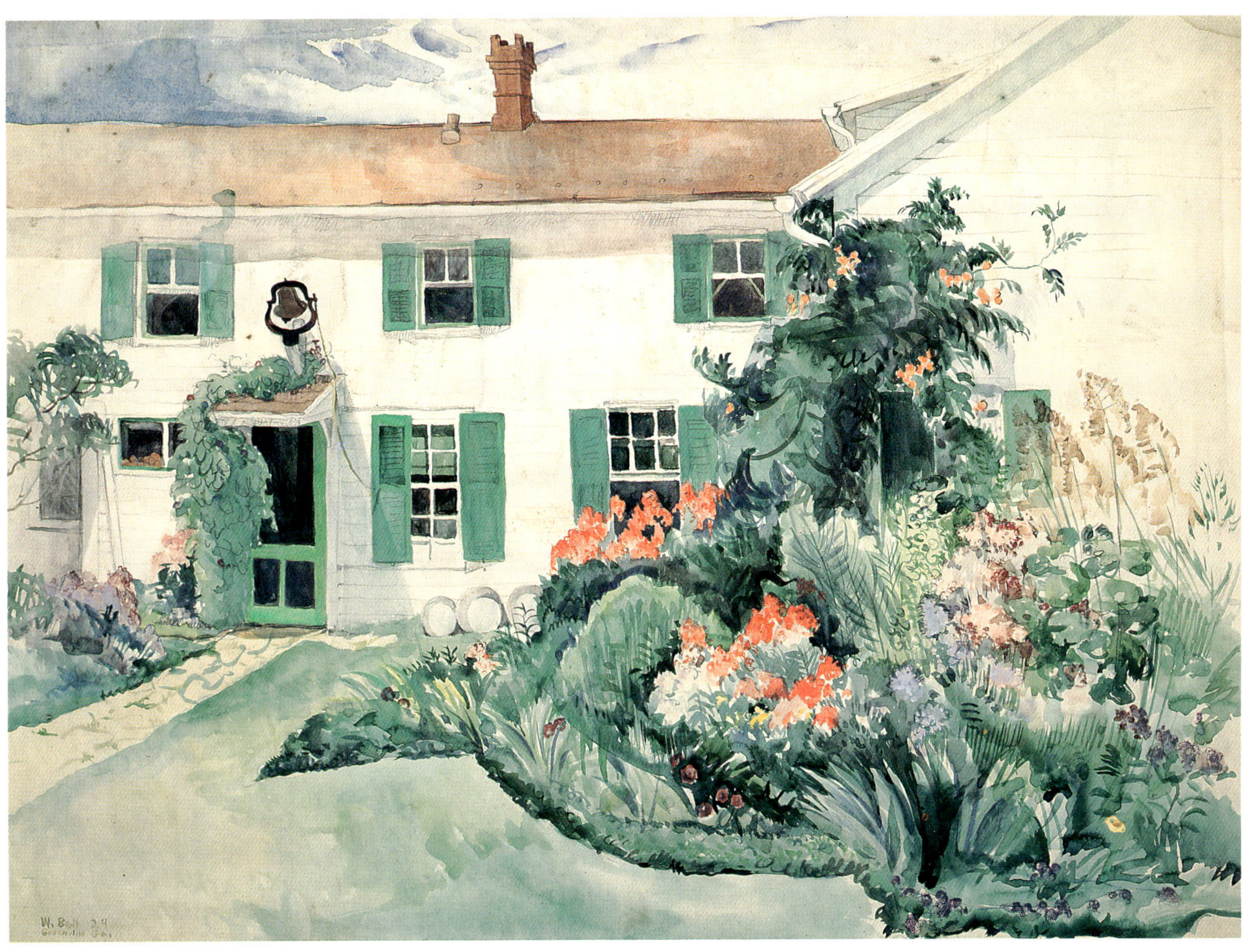

Christopher Patrick Hussey Murphy

1869 – 1939

Born, Savannah, Georgia; apprenticed as a sign painter in his father's firm while still a youth; active in Savannah throughout his career; died in Savannah.

Souvenir of the Studio, Telfair Academy

1923

Watercolor on paper, 14 ½ x 9 ½ inches
1993.C0858

MURPHY'S HIGHLY PROLIFIC ARTISTIC OUTPUT SPRANG FROM HIS own family roots in a large commercial art concern. Initially trained as a sign painter, Murphy polished his skills as a specialty finish artisan, and then as an easel painter in an assortment of studio sessions, and summer classes with established northeastern artists. Feay Shellman has suggested that the seminal moment in Murphy's artistic life occurred when he first viewed John Singer Sargent's watercolors at the Brooklyn Museum in 1909: "Sargent's strongest influence on Murphy was in the selection and composition of subject matter. The painters shared a fascination with the effects of light on architectural and sculptural objects."

The linkage between Sargent and Murphy is a fascinating one. Murphy is known to have copied many of Sargent's watercolors from on-site viewings and from his large collection of books on the American Impressionist master. Sargent made his living painting portraits but expressed his soul in his watercolors, which are often best in the sparkling evocations of light and shadow played out against elegantly solid background detail.

Yet Murphy was more than just a Sargent imitator. Whether from distance, exposure or indigenous talent, Murphy's watercolors project a personal spirit just as vivid as that of his expatriate hero. His figural studies often capture the spontaneous vitality which eludes many in a studio setting even as his floral still-life works have the wavering illusiveness of John Lafarge.

Still, this studio work was chosen for the particular manner in which the randomly placed objects, conveying an air of chaotic creativity, vie with the highly ordered atmosphere created by the deep rich color, and the tightly arranged background. Though nodding to Sargent in intent, they achieve a personal mastery of earnest ambition.

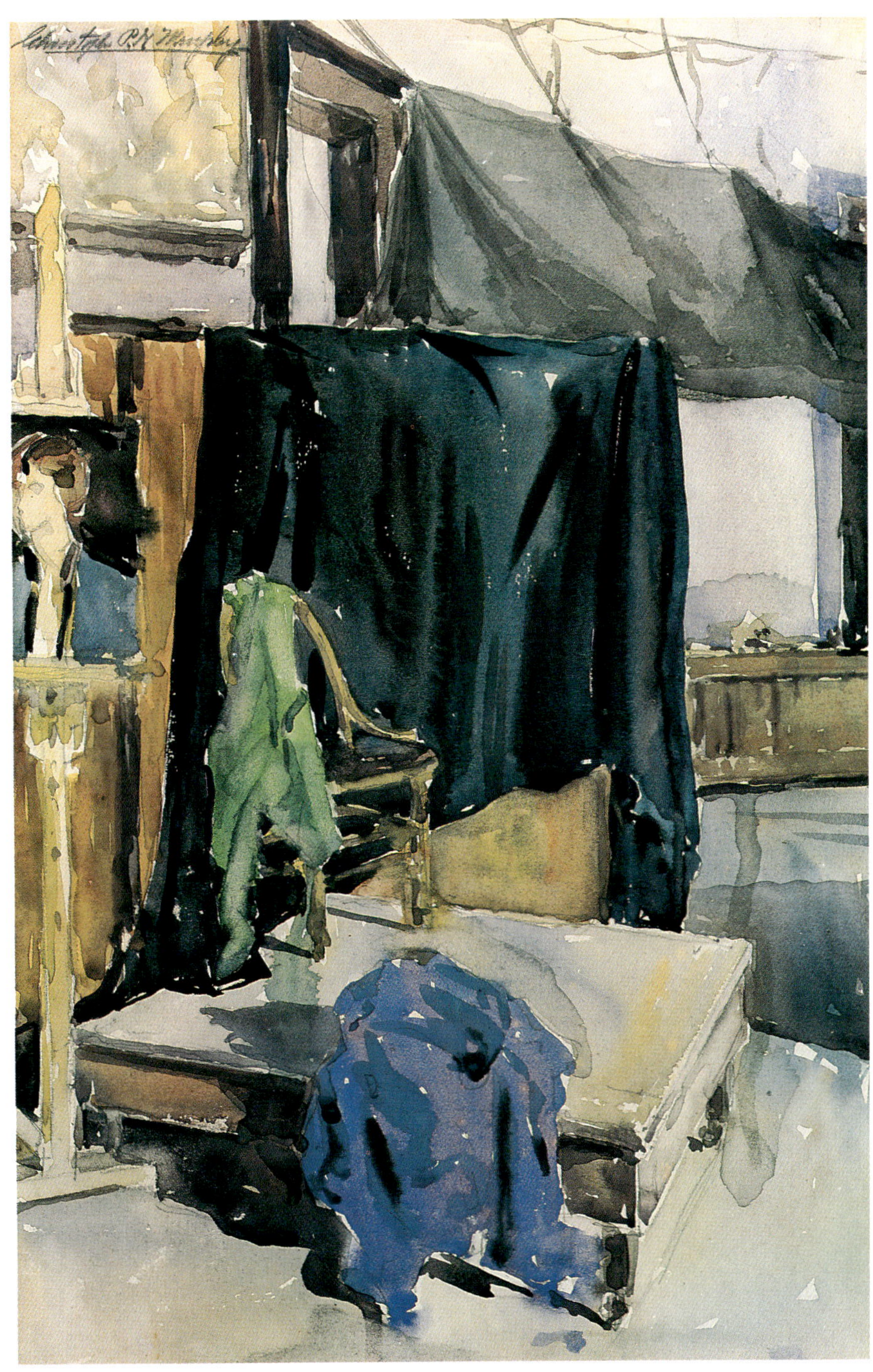

Angela Gregory

1903 – 1990

Born, New Orleans; studied with Ellsworth Woodward at Newcomb College, Tulane University, New Orleans, 1922, with Charles Keck in New York, 1923, and at the Academie de la Grande Chaumiere in Paris, France in the late '20s; active in New Orleans throughout her career; died in New Orleans.

Young Man in Shorts, Leaning

c. 1928

Sepia chalk on paper, 24 x 15½ inches
1990.086

ANGELA GREGORY'S MOTHER WAS THE ARTIST/DESIGNER SELINA Bres Gregory, whose Newcomb pottery work, as well as her painting and drawing activities, created a decisively formative environment for the young artist. Selina Gregory was also known as a lively individual, whose works often took on a humorous tone. Throughout her life, Angela Gregory displayed many of the same qualities in her own delightful sculpture and decorative work.

After some early training with Ellsworth Woodward at Newcomb, Gregory studied in New York with Charles Keck, an assistant to Augustus St. Gaudens. She then returned to New Orleans and further work at Newcomb before studying in Paris at the Academie de la Grande Chaumiere with the French academic Antoine Bourdelle.

In the best tradition of the Ecole des Beaux Arts, Gregory, as a sculptor, received superb training in life drawing. An ability to render the human form in two dimensions was seen as a foundation for sculptural work, especially in capturing stance, and in learning to model and contour anatomical features.

Upon her return from France, Gregory exhibited many of the drawings she completed while in Bourdelle's atelier. Among those were a group of drawings of young French schoolboys, posed with paint sticks or leaning against the studio wall, but always in configurations which demanded a sure grasp of curvilinear design. These particular drawings show subjects with the rather fey air of *fin de siecle* dandies of the Proustian variety. Lounging about, smoking, and sporting their best nautical attire, their languid poses have been captured by Gregory in a masterful way, one which eludes, amuses, and defies.

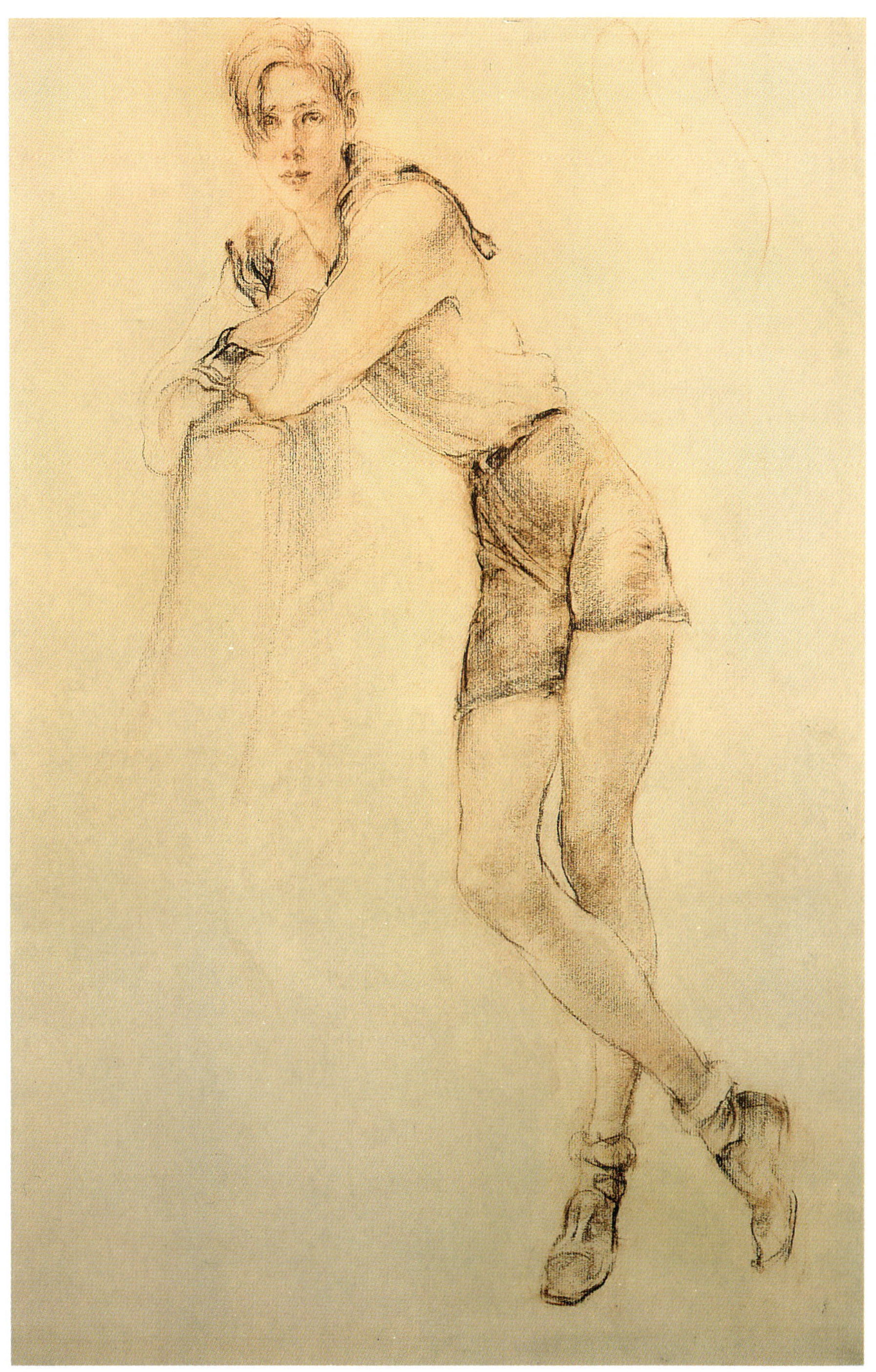

Edwin A. Harleston

1882 – 1931

Born, Charleston, South Carolina; studied at the Boston Museum of Fine Arts with Edmund C. Tarbell and Frank W. Benson; active in Charleston throughout his career; died in Charleston.

The Teacher

1926

Graphite on paper, 10½ x 14½ inches
1993.C0102

FOLLOWING HIS TRAINING AT THE BOSTON MUSEUM SCHOOL, Harleston returned to Charleston where he worked for his father in the family funeral home business. After the First World War, he developed an extensive clientele of black portrait subjects sufficient to enable him and his wife, the painter Elsie Harleston, to open a studio in 1922. During the rest of his career, Harleston gained considerable note as a sensitive and accomplished portraitist, including winning the Alain Locke Prize for portraiture from the Harmon Foundation shortly before his death.

Harleston's early education, at the Avery Institute and Atlanta University, was a manifestation of the missionary efforts of a variety of groups, both black and white, including the American Missionary Association. That experience, combined with his talents as an artist in charcoal, directly relate to the work at hand.

The Teacher recalls the paternalistic agenda of Harry Roseland and other apologist artists of the late nineteenth century, who often depicted black subjects in a condescending light. In Roseland's art the black subject seldom rises beyond earnest narrative intent to achieve a self-actualized position of personal authority and success. Harleston's depiction of a white teacher working with two elderly black students confounds the sensibility of a demanding, politically correct age.

But Harleston's agenda seems far more benign upon reflection. In the works of Roseland, William Aiken Walker and Edward Lamson Henry, the black subject is seldom seen in an attentive or enabling role. Here, the centrist position of the white teacher is balanced by the enclosing presence of the elderly black students who lean over the reading material with rapt interest. While the air of condescension cannot be dismissed, the earnest intent of the teacher cannot be disputed. Nor can the actual learning process be discounted as a means to end an ancient and oppressive system by the empowering ability to read, to comprehend and to express articulately.

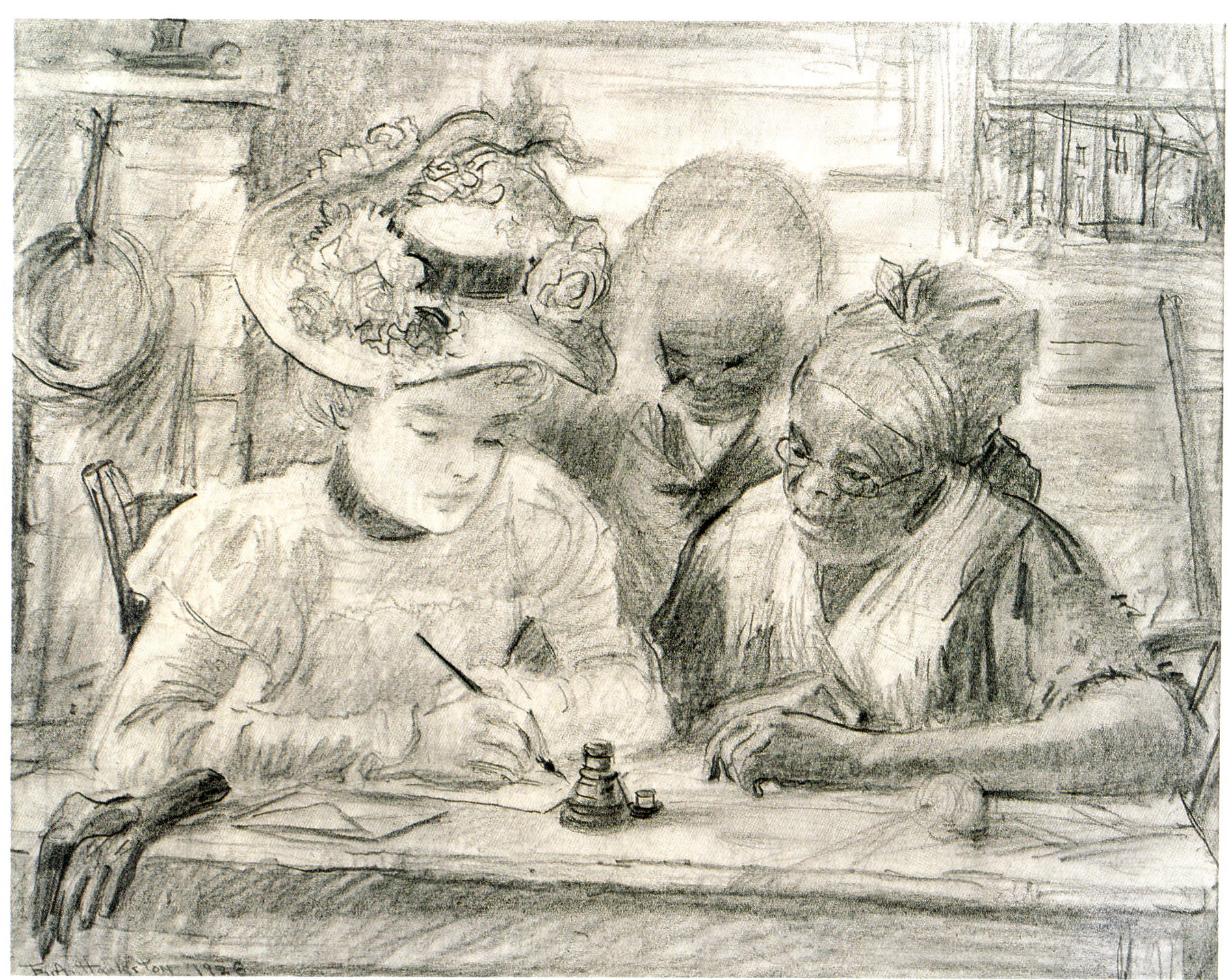

*Ella Sophonisba
Hergesheimer*

1873 – 1943

*Born, Allentown, Pennsylvania; studied with William
Merritt Chase and Cecilia Beaux at Pennsylvania
Academy of Fine Arts; active in Nashville, Tennessee,
1907-1943; died, Nashville.*

Mountain Landscape – River Bridge

c. 1930

Watercolor on paper, 10 x 13 ½ inches
1989.01.074

ELLA HERGESHEIMER'S SUPERB ACCOMPLISHMENTS AS PORTRAITIST,
still-life painter, and landscape artist in a variety of media reflect her
heritage as a great-great-granddaughter of Charles Willson Peale.
Whatever native talent she had was certainly honed by her formal
training with some of the master artists of the day.

Miss Hergesheimer made her living from painting portraits in
the warmly colored, grand manner tradition of the nineteenth
century, a talent which insured her constant employment from the
Nashville ascendancy. While nothing in these portraits suggests that
artistic vision is being sacrificed to a conservative clientele, they can
hardly be considered avant garde.

To glimpse her more progressive style one has to look at the
still-life art and the landscapes in watercolor. The vivid immediacy of
her still-life work recalls the Peale neo-classical sensibility expanded
by a rich, deep color in the art deco idiom. Above all, her watercolors
confirm a remarkable statement she made about the post-
impressionist generation in France. In an undated interview with a
Nashville newspaper she observed, "they have done something
wonderful for us. They have given us design which in a great
measure was lost by the impressionists, but which the great masters
of the past always had."

We may see this particular watercolor as a manifestation of that
belief. Where the impressionist would have chosen to obscure and
enhance the actual lines of the landscape view with bridge,
Hergesheimer has brilliantly affirmed their presence. Beneath the
staccato brushwork and strong color the parallel planes and strong
juxtaposition of foreground/midground/background recedes from the
inviting aperture of the picture plane. Even as we look with great
depth into this scene of glowing foliage and plunging river palisades,
our eye is distracted, as it would be in nature, by the movement and
variety alive in the enticing surrounds.

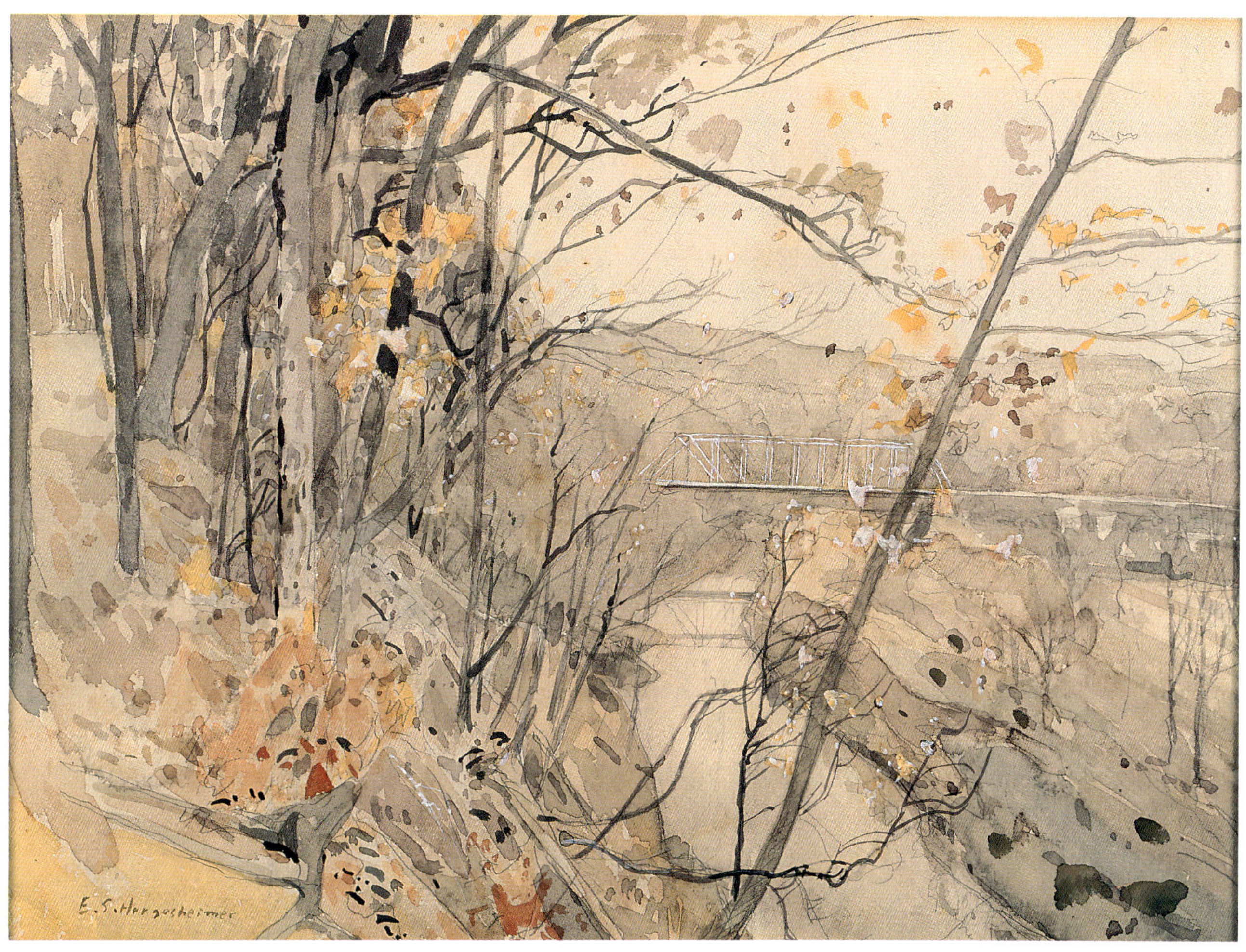

Alfred Heber Hutty

1877–1954

Born, Grand Haven, Michigan; studied at Art Students League Summer School in Woodstock, New York, with Birge Harrison, 1907; active in Charleston, South Carolina, 1919-1954; died, Woodstock.

Young Lady with Bouquet of Flowers

c. 1930

Watercolor on paper, 14 ½ x 12 inches
1993.C0180

ALFRED HUTTY'S CONTRIBUTIONS TO THE CHARLESTON RENAISSANCE account for one of the most important cross-cultural linkages in the history of painting in the South. By the time Hutty appeared in Charleston in the early 1920s, he was a well established painter and print-maker. An active participant in the Woodstock colony, he brought an air of formal training and first rate technique to a locale whose artists were either self-taught or informally trained. His professional presence and contacts greatly encouraged the Charleston artists. He was a major element in the climate of taste which produced such artists as Alice Smith and Elizabeth Verner, while fostering the articulate observations of the local scene which can be seen in the works of well known artists like Andree Ruellan and lesser known painters like Carrie Stubbs.

Many of these artists chose to depict black subjects in genre settings. The tone and style of these works reflect a complex blend of sincere social concern, genuine affection for an outsider group whose folkways were both compatible to and highly appealing for a bohemian imagination, and obvious, unfortunate, and persistently condescending stereotypes. Sorting out these agendas is made more difficult by the enduring inability to segregate flesh, bone and idiom in any art subject.

Hutty seems to have regarded the black subjects of Charleston with the genuine sensitivity of an outsider fascinated by the visual possibilities in the pose and manners of a charmingly distinctive sub-culture. The extant evidence shows he made hundreds of drawings of blacks on the street, at play and at work. These drawings, and the watercolors based on them, exist in the middle ground between mere caricature of the type practiced quite often by William Aiken Walker, and the more sensitive, realist efforts of subsequent generations of artists, black and white.

Young Woman with a Bouquet of Flowers is an appreciative image, one in which the flowers gathered up in the hands of the beautiful black woman enhance the thoughtful, pensive distance which Hutty has created. Whether social document or fleeting glance, it portrays a human being at a tentative moment, and it is the humanistic spirit of that moment which is best conveyed.

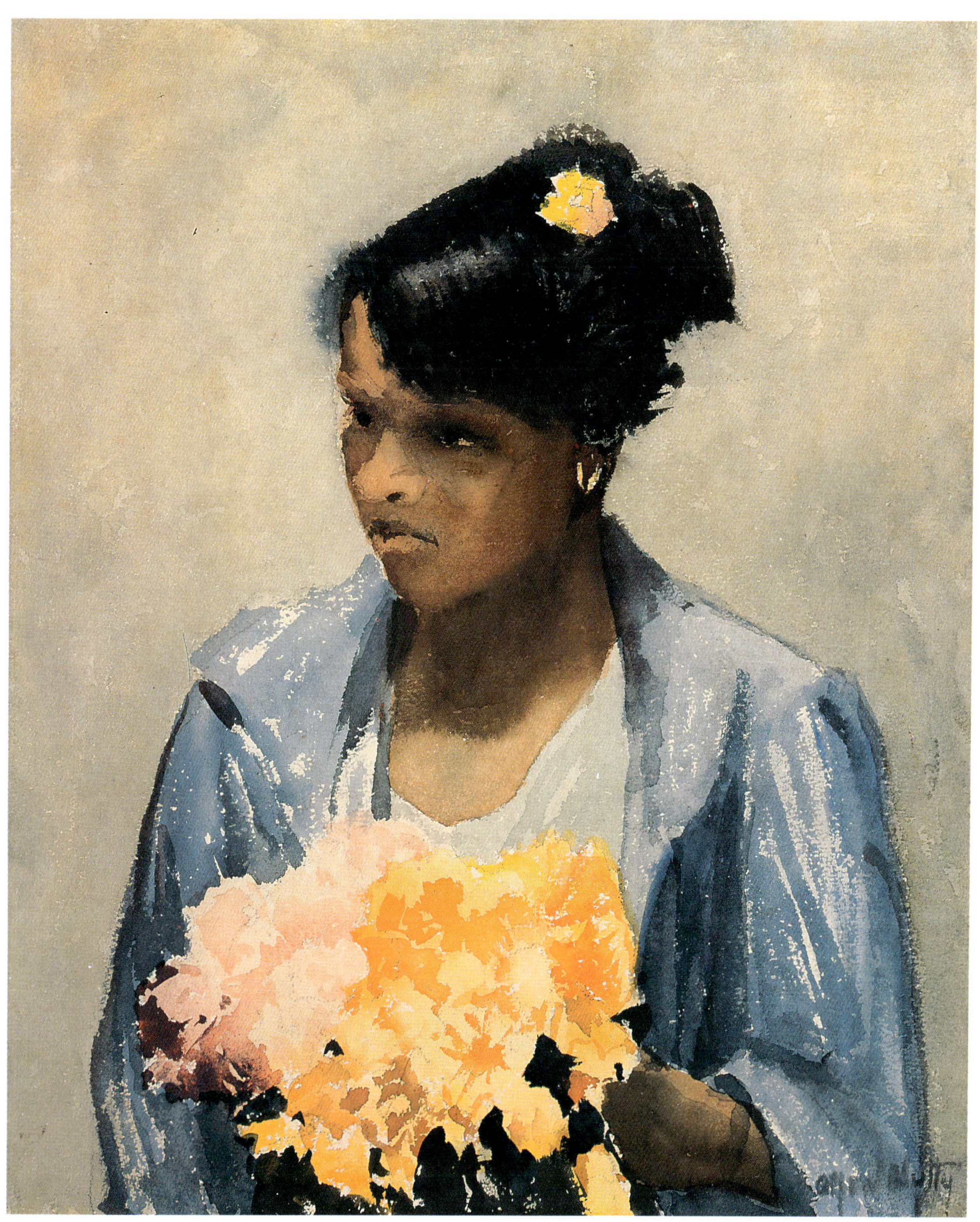

Paul Ninas

1903 – 1964

Born, Cape Girardeau, Missouri; studied, University of Nebraska, Robert College at Constantinople, the Royal Academy of Vienna, the Beaux Arts Academy, Paris, France, and in the atelier of Andre L'Hote, Paris, c.1920-1924; active in New Orleans, 1932-1968; died, New Orleans.

Swamp Scene

c. 1935

Watercolor on paper, 15 ¾ x 12 inches
1989.05.264

NINAS WAS SUCH A COLORFUL YOUNG CHARACTER, TEARING ABOUT on freighters in the Caribbean, visiting Gertrude Stein and Isadora Duncan in Paris, and finally landing in the French Quarter of New Orleans, where his most bohemian displays found a more than welcome, sophisticated audience. As he matured, Ninas, like his contemporaries and colleagues in the Arts and Crafts Club, John McCrady and Will Henry Stevens, was on the cutting edge of the Southern modernist movement. After he viewed an exhibition of Pablo Picasso's works at the Isaac Delgado Museum in 1940, his art would take on an increasingly cubist, vaguely non-objective format.

During the previous fifteen years, however, Ninas' style evokes the spirit of the post-impressionists – especially Gauguin with whose life style he doubtless identified – laid over a design sensibility distinctly derived from Cezanne. During his first ten years in New Orleans, he slowly moved out of representation and toward the analytic cubist style, with subtle coloration used to achieve a sense of mass and modeling, and with the same obvious, clean, geometric line giving the entire work an overall unity.

This drawing of the swamps is from that period. Unlike A. J. Drysdale, or the Woodwards for that matter, Ninas does not essay the murky lowlands as a painterly exercise in atmospherics. Instead, the sharp lines of the foliage and the density of the undergrowth prove to be vehicles for strong and rather unusual blends of color. The jagged edges and lurching proximity of the mass to the picture plane create a confrontational quality, clearly two dimensional.

"The choicer spirits want color and form," Ninas once told a reporter. "Of what significance is a 'speaking' likeness if it has no emotional satisfaction?"

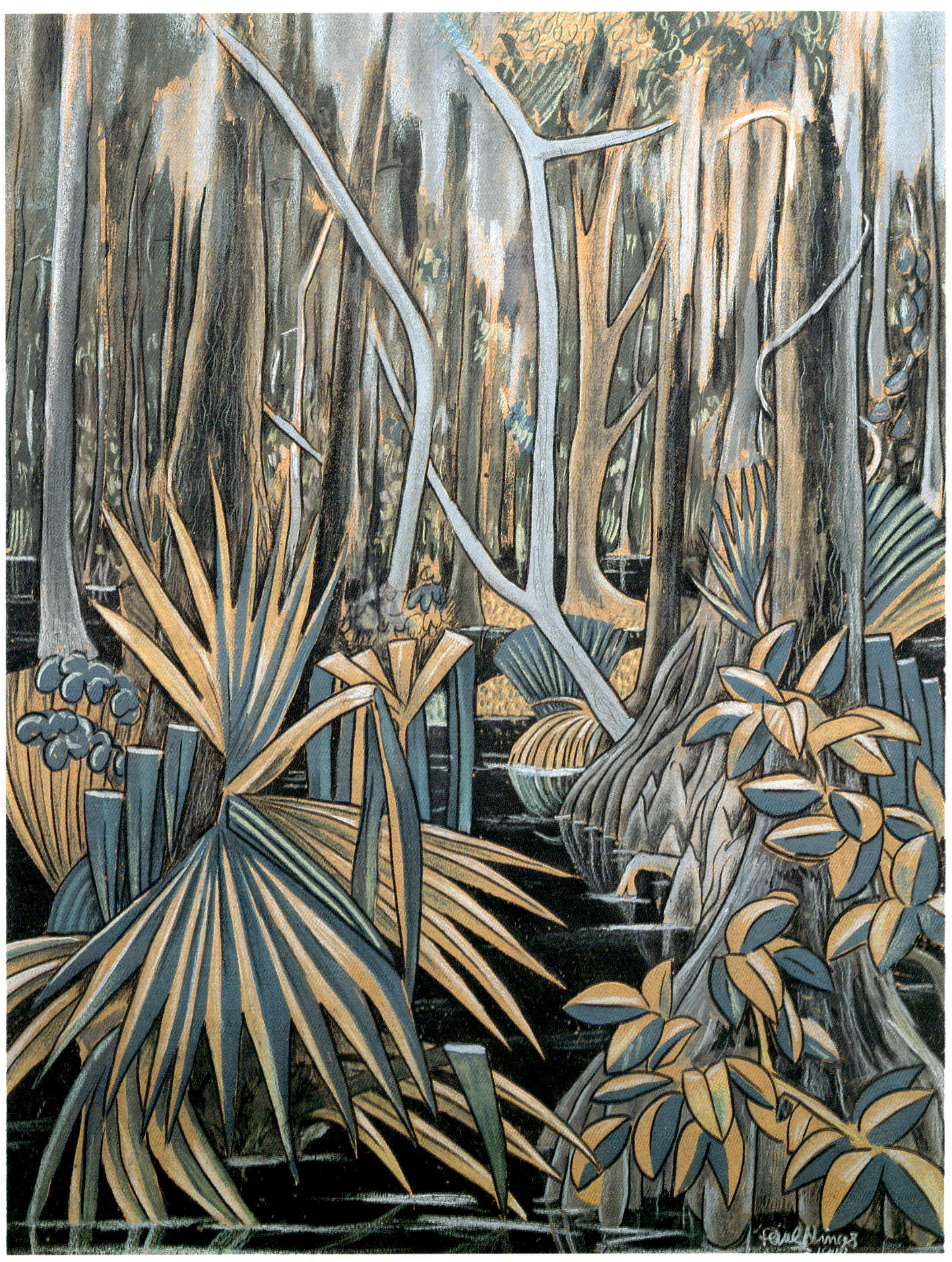

Elizabeth White

1883 – 1976

Born, Sumter, South Carolina; studied with Wayman Adams at the Pennsylvania Academy of Fine Arts prior to World War I; active in Charleston and Sumter throughout her life; died, Sumter.

White Roses and a Cigarette

c. 1935

Watercolor on paper, 19 ¾ x 18 ¾ inches
1993.C0189

VERY EARLY IN HER RATHER LONG AND PRODUCTIVE LIFE, WHITE IS thought to have been inspired to pursue a career as a printmaker of Southern genre scenes by the likely marketability of these works. Subsequently she acquired first rate skills in dry point and aquatint from Alfred Hutty. During the '30s, when there was such a pronounced taste for prints in the arts and crafts tradition, she achieved considerable note, which culminated in her major exhibition at the Smithsonian's Division of Graphic Arts in 1939.

Be that as it may, time has been much kinder to her gorgeously tonal watercolors and pastels. The prints are hostages of the quaint attitudes of an ever more distant past, well stated and atmospheric evocations of trees and black subject matter difficult to distinguish from others of their type by masters as accomplished as Alfred Hutty or the lesser known students of the Carolina Art Association.

But Elizabeth White's work in watercolor reveals her subtle abilities in close color harmonics. Any successful practitioner of the watercolor medium understands its distinction as an expressive vehicle, especially when compared to oil. With oil, even oil in the impressionist idiom, laying down and building up paint, brushstroke and color juxtaposition are demanding techniques despite such seemingly spontaneous effects.

With watercolor, mastery is most often achieved in aqueous blendings which float across the surface of the picture plane. *White Roses and a Cigarette* is a masterwork of intrigue and intimacy, an evasive still-life which invites the viewer into the midst of a conversation even as we look about to see the guests who are nowhere to be found. Who, after all, lit the match?

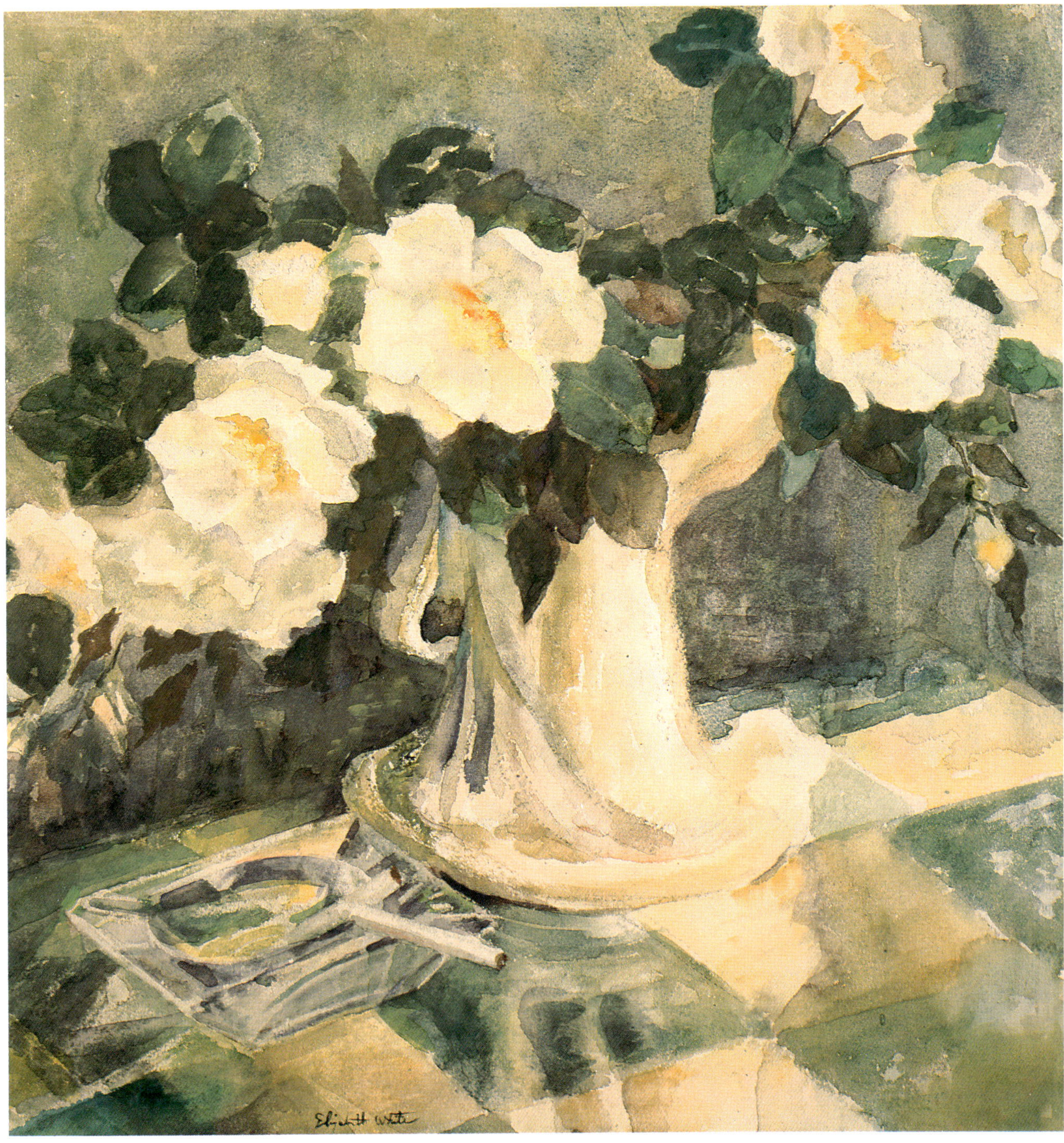

Nell Choate Jones

1879 – 1981

Born, Hawkinsville, Georgia; studied, c.1925, at the Adelphia Academy, Brooklyn, New York; intermittently active in the South, especially in Georgia, 1936-1956; died, Brooklyn.

Cotton Blooms

c. 1936

Mixed media on paper, 21⅜ x 17⅞ inches
1993.C0377

ALTHOUGH NELL CHOATE JONES LEFT THE SOUTH WHILE STILL A very little girl when her family sought better economic opportunity in Brooklyn, her love of the red clay hills of Georgia never left her. She actually took up the pursuit of art later in life, after teaching for many years. At the instigation of her husband, the etcher and artist Eugene Jones, she began to work in oil sometime early in 1927, enjoying a certain immediate recognition.

Jones's first work in oils was painted in the impressionist style, an affectation she enhanced by a study tour abroad to Fontainbleu in 1929. Thereafter she exhibited a great deal, becoming something of a legend in the women's art organizations of the New York area. Her ceaseless energies sustained her quite happily well past her one-hundredth year, a time when she could honestly tell a reporter she "never felt old."

During the 1930s, Jones began to make trips back to her native Georgia, visiting relatives and friends, and the old sites of her youth which she so treasured. The works these visits inspired represent some of the artist's finest achievements. One superb oil, *Georgia Red Clay,* has a power which was noted in a review of her Georgia work in an undated newspaper clipping following an exhibition of that subject matter. "Miss Jones's color is keyed to the murky red of the Georgia soil – deep, somber, earthy tones heightened by strong whites and black."

Cotton Blooms is also certainly from this period, a time in which the art of Nell Jones has the strongly defined compositional lead-lines of American scene painting of the regionalist type. There is powerful presence in this still-life which seems to press forward upon the viewer, growing before our eyes, taking on great solidity of form.

Very late in her life, Nell Jones made a simple statement of faith. She survived so long because she "never worried about anything" and always had a comfortable, reassuring feeling "there was always something waiting for me. Something would just come along and offer itself. It wasn't anything really, I just had to get there."

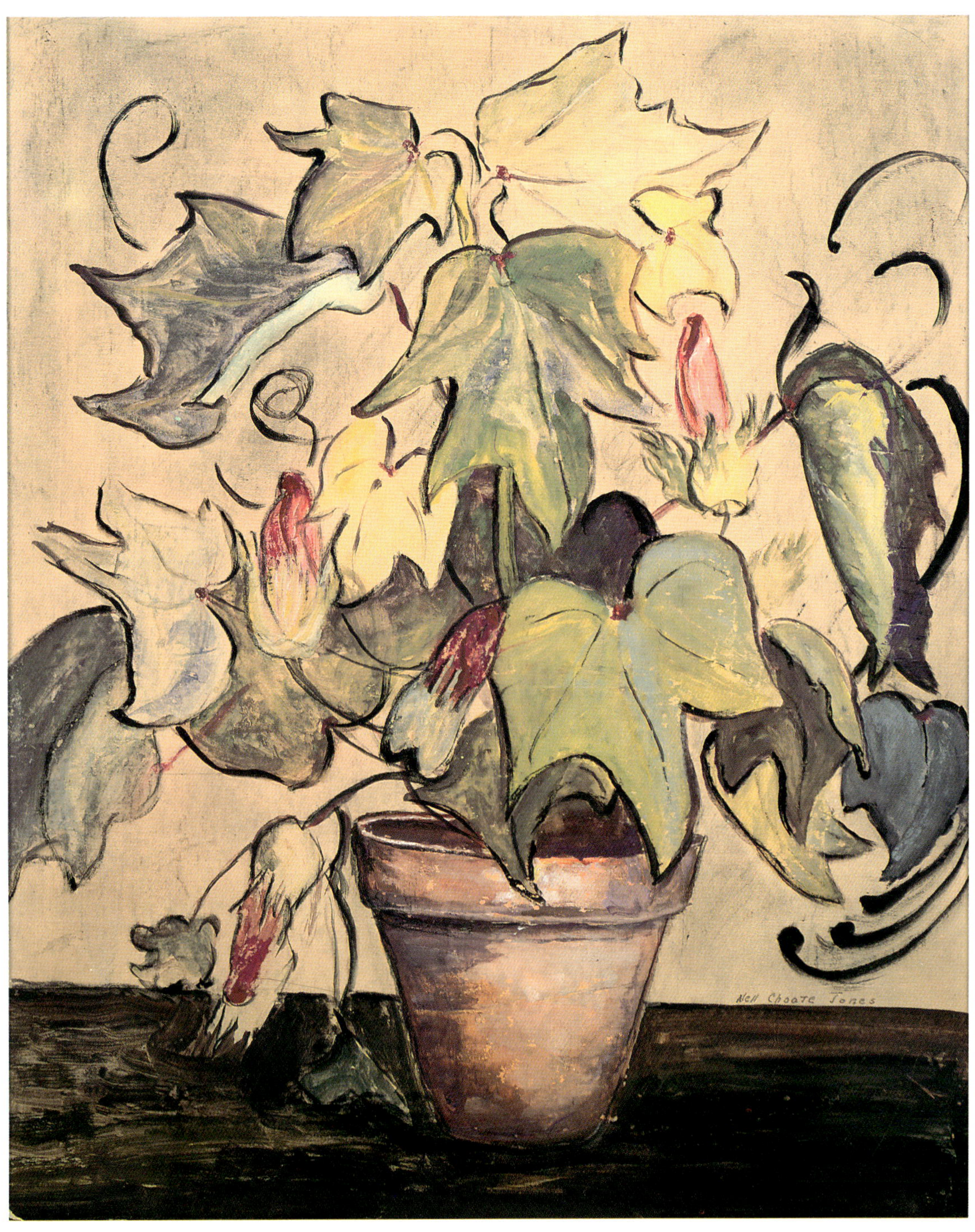

Aiden Lassell Ripley

1896 – 1969

Born, Wakefield, Massachusetts; studied at the School of the Museum of Fine Arts, Boston, with Edmund Charles Tarbell, Philip Hale, and Frank Weston Benson, 1920-1922; active as a seasonal itinerant sporting artist in Florida, South Carolina and Georgia at intermittent periods from 1936 to c.1965; died, Lexington, Massachusetts.

Study for "Duck Shooting"

c. 1940

Graphite on paper, 9 x 13 ½ inches
1993.C0110

RIPLEY'S COOL AND TERRIBLY ELEGANT COMPOSITIONS ARE REDEEMED from mere illustration by his highly accomplished figural drawing, placing his subjects in settings which may be idealized but do achieve a sense of place. As a sporting artist, he attained a national stature augmented by his works in the South which rank among the finest of their kind.

A. L. Ripley did not begin his career as a sporting artist. He was trained by Philip Hale in the Boston Impressionist style, which he perfected in his association with Frank Weston Benson and William McGregor Paxton. After his return from the first world war, Ripley painted and sold landscape works.

By all accounts, it was the Depression which turned Ripley's attention toward sporting art. An avid hunter since his youth, he was often out on the trail of upland birds in the company of his longtime friend, Guido Perera. During one of their treks, Perera suggested that Ripley "might well turn his brush, in part at least, to a subject in which he was by instinct a master – upland game birds and upland shooting as well as waterfowl." Following his first exhibit of this subject matter at the Guild of Boston Artists in 1930, he became widely known. Following his association with the Sportsman's Gallery of Art and Books in New York in 1936, he made several painting and sketching expeditions to the South.

Perera often accompanied his friend Ripley on hunting outings, and described his keen instinct for spotting birds. Seldom relying upon "that rarest of all creatures, a good grouse dog," Ripley would quietly point them out himself. "Aiden," said Perera, "you think like a bird and you have taught me more hunting craft and pointed out more interesting features of nature than I could have imagined."

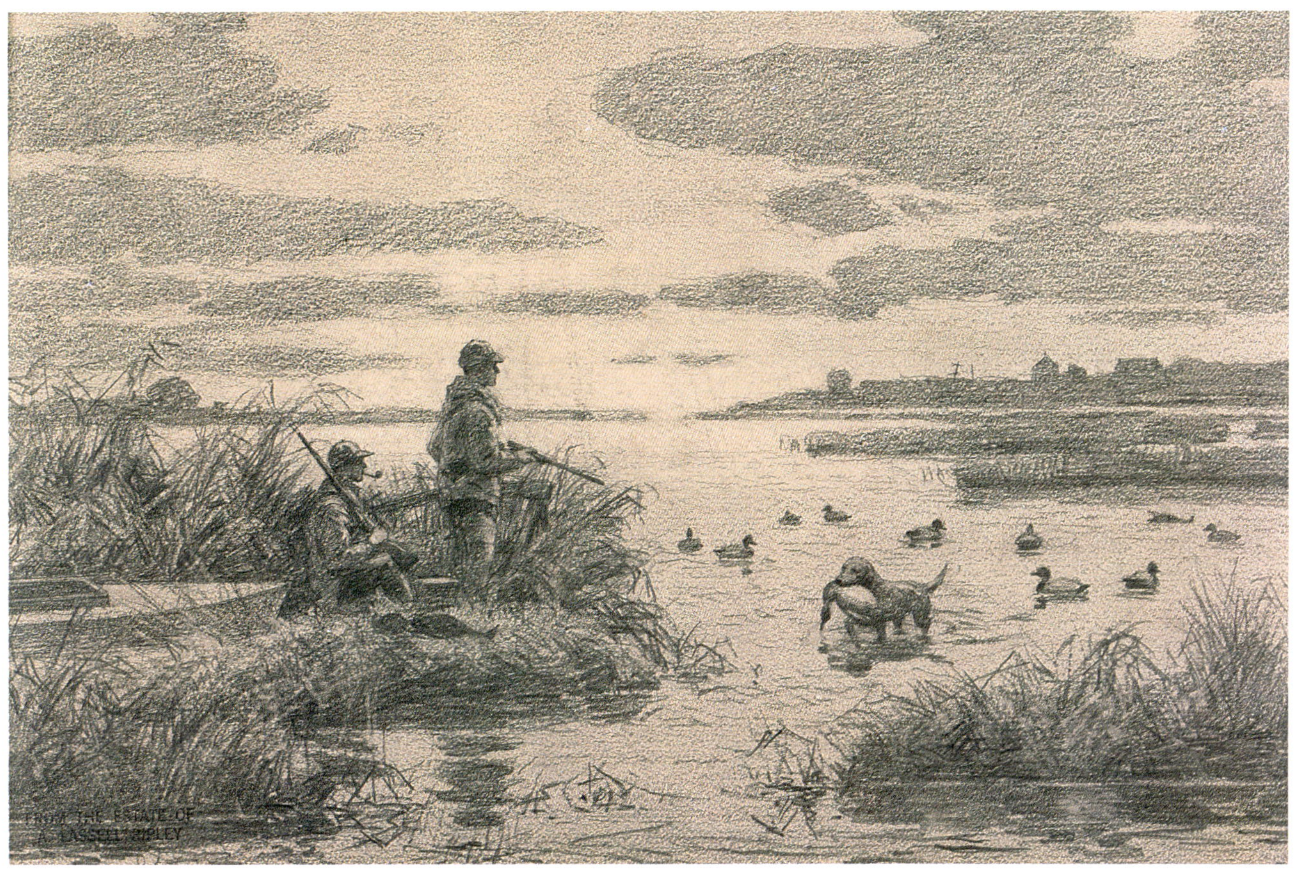
FROM THE ESTATE OF
A. LASSELL RIPLEY

Alexander Brook

1898 – 1980

Born, Brooklyn, New York; studied at the Art Students League with Kenneth Hayes Miller, Frank Vincent Dumond, and George Bridgeman, 1913-1917; active in Savannah, Georgia, 1938-1945; died, Sag Harbor, New York.

Study for Twentieth Century Ruin

c. 1940

Graphite on Paper, 16 x 22 ½ inches
1993.C0365

AS A PRODUCT OF THE ART STUDENTS LEAGUE DURING KENNETH HAYES Miller's tenure as a drawing master, Brook was well versed in the tradition of American realism and naturalism expressed by the artists of the Ashcan School. Between the wars, Brook was one of the major figures in American art, heralded as a pre-eminent realist for his sensuous female figurative studies and for his urban genre scenes.

Throughout these years, Brook was married to the artist/writer Peggy Bacon, whose witty prints and paintings were often clever caricatures of the milieu in which the Brooks moved in New York. It almost seems as though their styles played to each other, Brook's intensity softened by Bacon's wit, but both sharing, and perhaps enhancing, a fine sense of line in design.

By the late 1930s, the Brook marriage was deteriorating, and even as Brook himself won the prestigious Carnegie Prize in 1939, the climate of taste in American art was shifting from academic realism to more experimental non-objective styles of the type which swept the international art scene in the decade prior to the second world war.

Following his separation from Peggy Bacon, Brook moved to Savannah where he rented an apartment and began to explore the poorer sides of town for realist subject matter. Throughout his Savannah stay he was enormously productive, making frequent drawings of street life and the surrounding countryside, while painting portraits and genre scenes finely attuned to the atmosphere of the old Southern town which time had forgotten.

This drawing of a house in ruins seems to have been made during a critical turning point in Brook's life and in the life of the cultural world he had briefly dominated. Behind him lay a kind of golden youth. Ahead, war, divorce, and radical social change. By the time Brook left Savannah the world he had known was over; his reputation and career were in a decline from which they would not recover in his lifetime.

Study for Twentieth Century Ruin may not be a parable, but the decay and collapse of a well wrought structure with pronounced historical overtones may have appealed to the sensitivities of this highly accomplished, and soon to be disappointed, man.

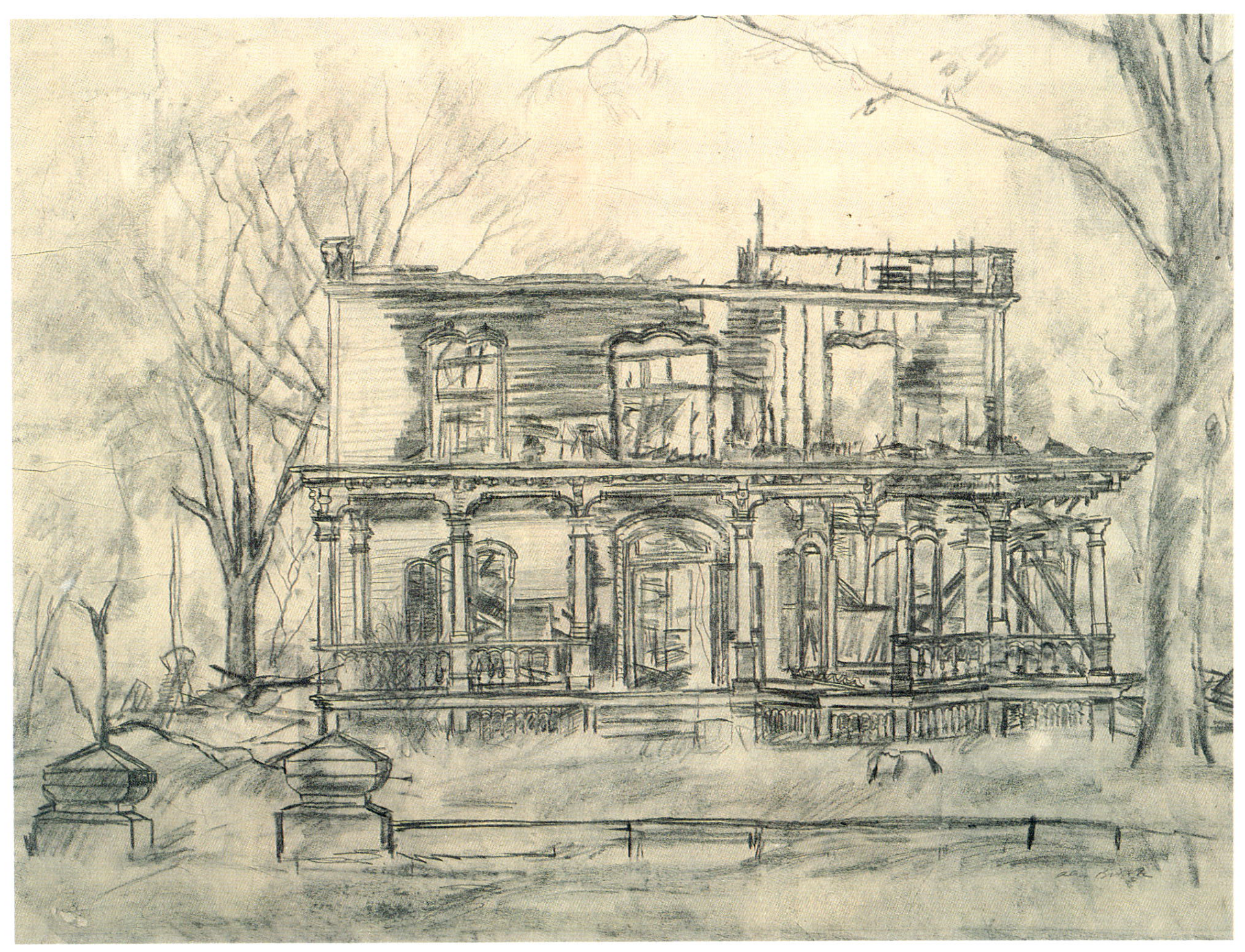

Elizabeth O'Neill Verner

1883 – 1979

Born, Charleston, South Carolina; studied at the Pennsylvania Academy of the Fine Arts, Philadelphia, 1903-1904; at the Central School of Art in London, 1930; and with the Japanese printmaker Rakasan, in Kyoto, Japan, 1937; active in Charleston throughout her career; died in Charleston.

The Flower Vendor

c. 1945

Pastel on silk, 27 ⅞ x 23 inches
1989.01.211

WHEN VERNER EMBARKED UPON HER CAREER AS AN ARTIST WHILE still a very young person, it was with that genteel spirit which characterizes the involvement of many women in the Arts and Crafts movement. However, when her husband died in 1925, leaving her with two young children to raise, Verner turned to her art as a means of support.

In order to survive, she painted the black flower vendors and street scenes and architecture of Charleston, as well as making a series of prints whose popularity has endured for three quarters of a century. As an artist of the Charleston Renaissance, she became one of the most familiar figures in the cultural life of the city, a renowned figure whose many achievements included illustrations for Dubose Heyward's "Porgy." A trenchant reactionary, she deplored all forms of modernism as "public self-deception."

Apart from her prints, Verner was perhaps best known for the pastel portraits, often on silk, which she painted of the local Charleston street vendors selling their flowers and baskets along the streets downtown. While they display her considerable skill in mastering a chalky medium on a slick surface, their depiction of black subject matter raises questions not unlike those posed by the genre paintings of William Aiken Walker.

Henry Louis Gates, Jr., a black art historian, has written of the visual traditions in painting black subject matter from the antebellum period down through the years following the second world war: "The black person was rarely dignified with individuality in works of art, because depictions of individuals would attest to the full range of variety of human characteristics and abilities."

In Verner's work, and images of this type are legion, there is a conflicting agenda of paternalism and social realism. Though wonderfully presented, it is difficult to find the humanity in this subject, beyond her tiring and poorly paid role as a kind of black Eliza Doolittle selling flowers to passing tourists seeking a scintillating moment of local color.

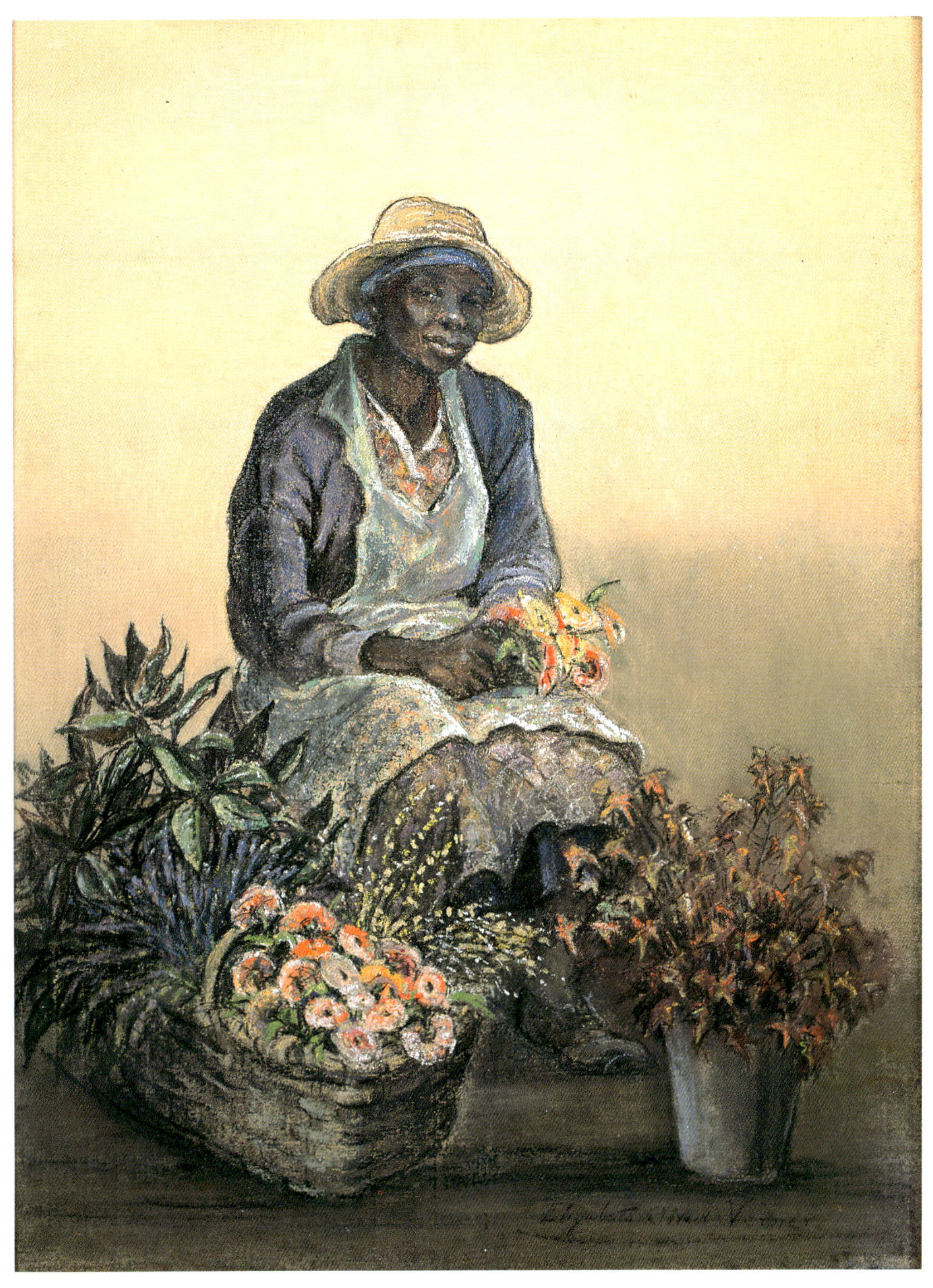

John McCrady

1911–1968

Born, Canton, Mississippi; studied, University of Mississippi, Pennsylvania Academy of Fine Arts, New Orleans Arts and Crafts Club, Art Students League, New York City; active in New Orleans, 1932-1968; died, New Orleans.

Cartoon for "Repatriated"

c. 1945

Pencil on paper, 18¾ x 25¾ inches
1989.05.259

FOR THE FIRST FIFTEEN YEARS OF HIS CAREER, JOHN MCCRADY, A white artist, painted the rural spiritual life and folkways of the black people he knew as a youth in Mississippi and Louisiana. His work during this period is very much in that spirit of narrative realism which one associates with the great regionalist painters of the American scene. Like Benton, Wood, and Curry, he was seeking to define in strident pictorial terms the very substance and texture of a world removed from the demeaning decay of urban economic depression and existential dislocation.

Regarding his goals, the artist was quite articulate: "I see in painting one way to express our age, the people and their surroundings, their philosophy of life, the emotional reason for their being – as well as my own destiny to thus interpret the meaning of life, as I see it, to those people who are my neighbors."

McCrady may have been the first artist whose reputation suffered because his work was viewed as politically incorrect. A reviewer for the left wing "Daily Worker," viewing an exhibition of the artist's work in 1946, deplored "the outright slander of the Negro people." This "slander" was perpetrated by McCrady's enthusiastic paintings of black religious life, combining myth and symbol in a folk frenzy not unlike that of Dubose Heyward's "Porgy." McCrady never returned to black subject matter thereafter.

However, at the time of the review, he had in progress a major work which viewed the impact of the end of the second world war on a black family. This drawing is a study for that painting, *Repatriated*, a warm and sympathetic portrait of a young black soldier returning to a rural homestead. Several variances between the painting and the drawing exist, most notably the presentation of the serviceman here, as a sailor in formal dress whites complete with flowing tie, while in the painting he appears as a rather dapper soldier in khaki.

Repatriated does beg those same questions which we may continue to ask of Southern art. It is true that the setting to which the serviceman returns is deplorable at best, a remnant of the impoverished existence of the rural sharecropper. Still, even as McCrady appropriates a trite and unfortunate metaphor, his figures have the musculature of survivors, and the happy family life which seems to await the young warrior is filled with a love that crosses color lines.

To understand and appreciate Southern art of this type may well take several more generations, until that time when we can look upon the melodrama of human life and find that all victims share the promise of love, just as all victors face the daily possibility of defeat.

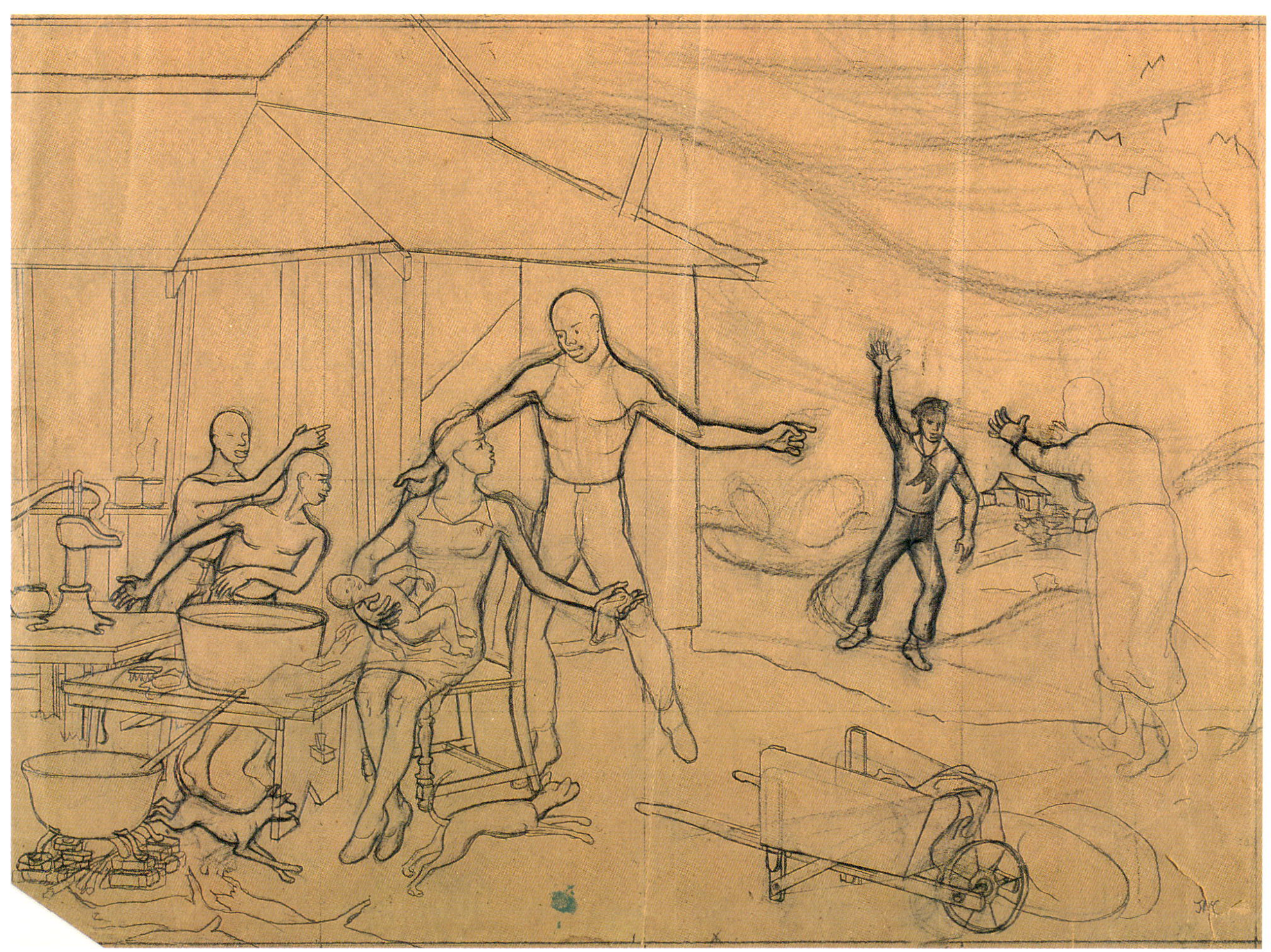

Hobson Pittman

1900 – 1972

Born, Epworth, North Carolina; studied at the Rouse Art School in Tarboro, North Carolina, at Pennsylvania State College and the Carnegie Institute, Pittsburgh; active in North and South Carolina throughout his career; died, Philadelphia.

Street Scene, Charleston

c. 1946

Pastel on sandpaper, 11½ x 14¾ inches
1993.C1249

EVAN TURNER, WRITING AT THE TIME OF HIS TENURE AS THE VERY distinguished Director of the Philadelphia Museum of Art, felt that Hobson Pittman was "a product of that curious other worldliness which for so many is the true nature of the South. He is very much of it, but significantly he broke from it. . . ." Turner, assessing Pittman's status as a Southern expatriate, maintains that "rather than pursue the conventional unimaginative life that was expected of him, he departed – more truthfully, he fled to the North" in order to begin his career as an artist.

Further illumination upon Turner's hypothesis, which makes Pittman sound like William Faulkner's character Quentin Compson as acted out by Holden Caulfield, reveals that the artist's mother, father, and sister, to whom he fled in Philadelphia, all died within a brief period of time prior to his eighteenth birthday. It doesn't seem far-fetched to imagine that this domino-effect mortality rate made a rather sobering impact upon his sense of self, art, and the mutability of all things.

While Pittman did live in the North, the works he created throughout his career have much of the same spirit of the past haunting the present that one reads in the writers of the Southern literary renascence. Writers like Allen Tate and Robert Penn Warren explored the meaning of a Southern past whose sense of place and social order, compounded by the ironies of racial conflict and paternalism, created seemingly irreconcilable conflicts in the contemporary Southern soul. Characters, in their poems, novels and plays, are neither old South gentry, nor liberated moderns. Instead, they dwell between two worlds, the one dead, the other struggling toward a birth or rebirth, which probably occurred in Birmingham and Selma in 1964.

This pastel is redolent of that "other worldliness" to which Turner alludes. In 1946 Pittman was commissioned by *Life* magazine to paint a series of interior views in Charleston. This pastel is an on-site work from that period. The shimmering waves of heat, the vivid colors of the structures themselves, and the vibrant intensity in mood achieve a visual unity evocative of the "Holy City" at high season.

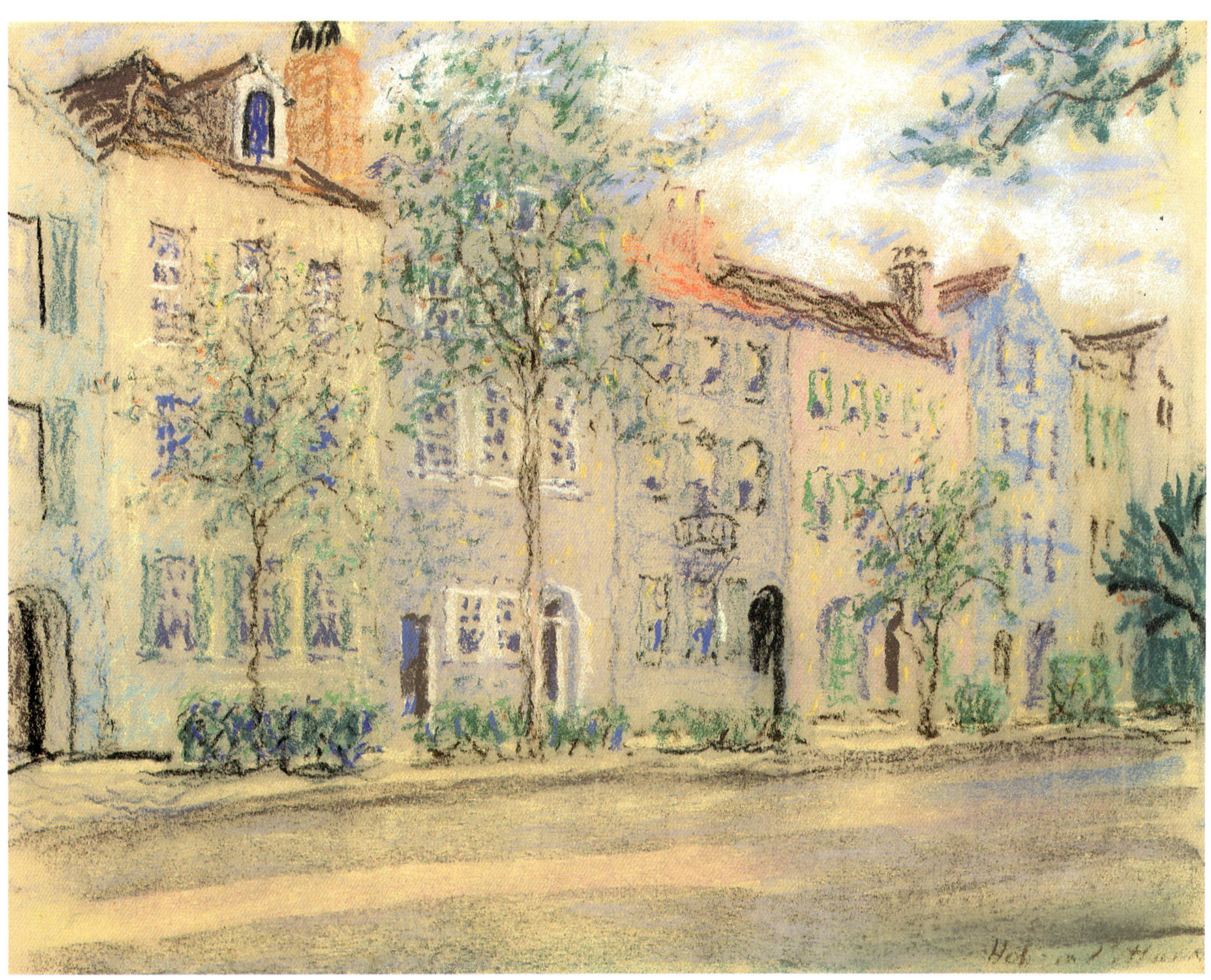

Adele Lemm

1904 – 1977

Born near Milwaukee, Wisconsin; studied at Sienna College, Memphis, Tennessee, with George and Henriette Obertauffer at the Memphis Academy of Arts, and at the Colorado Springs Fine Arts Center with Vaclav Vytlacil, 1951-1952; active in Memphis throughout her career; died in Memphis.

Island Houses

c. 1952

Pastel on paper, 20 ⅛ x 26 ⅛ inches
1989.01.103

LIKE MANY THOUGHTFUL ARTISTS OF THE MID–TWENTIETH CENTURY, Adele Lemm moved toward a non-objective style through a series of learning experiences that extended her visual awareness. At heart in her art, one is aware of the influence of Cezanne, that master of flat color application, whose schematic-like renderings break up the pictorial scene into compatible color variations laid down with a fairly broad brush.

Lemm's sensitivity to more avant-garde trends was almost certainly sharpened by her exposure, late in her career, to the teaching of Vaclav Vytlacil in Colorado Springs. For many years, that school had one of the most progressive art training programs in the West, inspiring several Southern artists of a later generation.

But the most important exposure Lemm may have had occurred during the summers she spent in the northeast, at Monhegan, Maine, and at Martha's Vineyard. While there, in the midst of large and vital art colonies, she produced some of her finest works. Many of these are beach and harbor scenes rendered in bright colors laid over a vaguely recognizable representational skeleton. Like an early cubist, she slavishly acknowledges the two-dimensionality of the picture plane, eschewing depth and perspective for a shimmering interaction of color.

Lemm lived and worked at a time when the opinions of the New York art scene loomed so large upon the modern imagination as to create a defensive, apologetic feel among many artists working elsewhere in the country. Guy Northrop, a feature writer for the Memphis "Commercial Appeal," noted in an article on the artist's New York showings, that "her paintings have nothing regional about them in style, technique or subject."

While it is somewhat unclear as to how regional non-objective painting might be characterized under such a posture, Lemm was well regarded by certain critics in New York. Northrop reports that one art review found Lemm's work to have "a clean airy quality and style cogently compatible with her interest in nature. Her thinly applied paint . . . contributes a breathing, ethereal role to compositions."

While that may be true, it is far more interesting to note that Lemm pursued an imaginative approach while living outside the recognized mainstream, a tribute to her insight as much as to her locale.

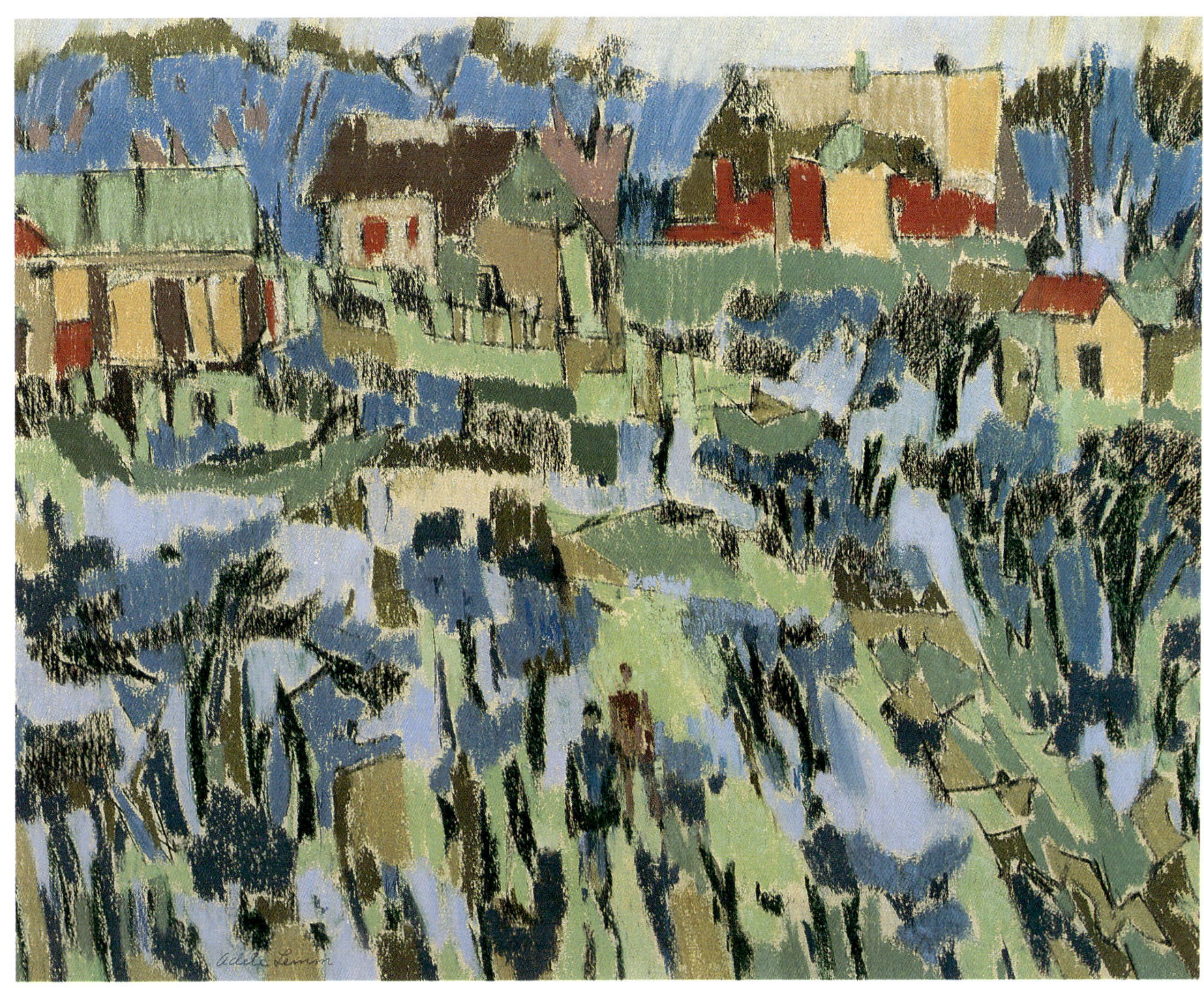

Nell Choate Shute

1896 –1966

Born, Athens, Georgia; studied at Hollins College in Virginia, and at the Parsons School of Design in New York City, during the 1920s; active in Atlanta, Georgia, throughout her career.

Working on the Railroad, Atlanta, Georgia

c. 1955

Watercolor and graphite on paper, 22½ x 30¾ inches
1993.C1186

NELL CHOATE SHUTE WAS THE PRODUCT OF A VERY TALENTED family whose other members included the painter Nell Choate Jones and the architect Ellamae League. Though born in Athens, Nell Choate was raised in Atlanta, where she spent most of her life. Like her contemporary, Mary Passailaigue, she attended Hollins College, but continued her art education at the Parsons School of Design, whose exacting technical standards and interest in the avant garde may account for certain experimental forms in the artist's work.

While still a very young woman, Nell Choate served with the Red Cross Motor Corps in World War I in the European Theater. While abroad she met Lt. William L. Plummer, whom she married and by whom she had one daughter. The marriage ended in divorce in 1932.

Her second marriage, to B. E. Shute, was very significant for her career. Shute was an artist who moved to Atlanta in 1928 to direct the art school associated with the fledgling High Museum of Art. After their marriage, Nell Shute traveled a great deal and frequently exhibited her works in national and regional competitions, including those organized by the Southern States Art League, and the National Academy of Design.

Shute's daughter, Beatrice Plummer Potts, often noted the artist's preference for watercolor in the biographical sketches of her mother she provided for various dealers and collectors. The Morris Museum's collection is particularly rich in those watercolors, thanks to the ceaseless collecting energies of the late Dr. Robert Powell Coggins. In many of the works, Shute employed a deep, rich palette, executed with a wavering brushstroke which gives them a tremendous presence enhanced by the frequent placement of the figure close to the picture plane. As can be seen in this work, however, Mrs. Shute had a lingering interest in areas of genre painting which can be associated with the American scene style of the 1930s. Here, the simple act of working on a railroad line is expanded into a colorful landscape.

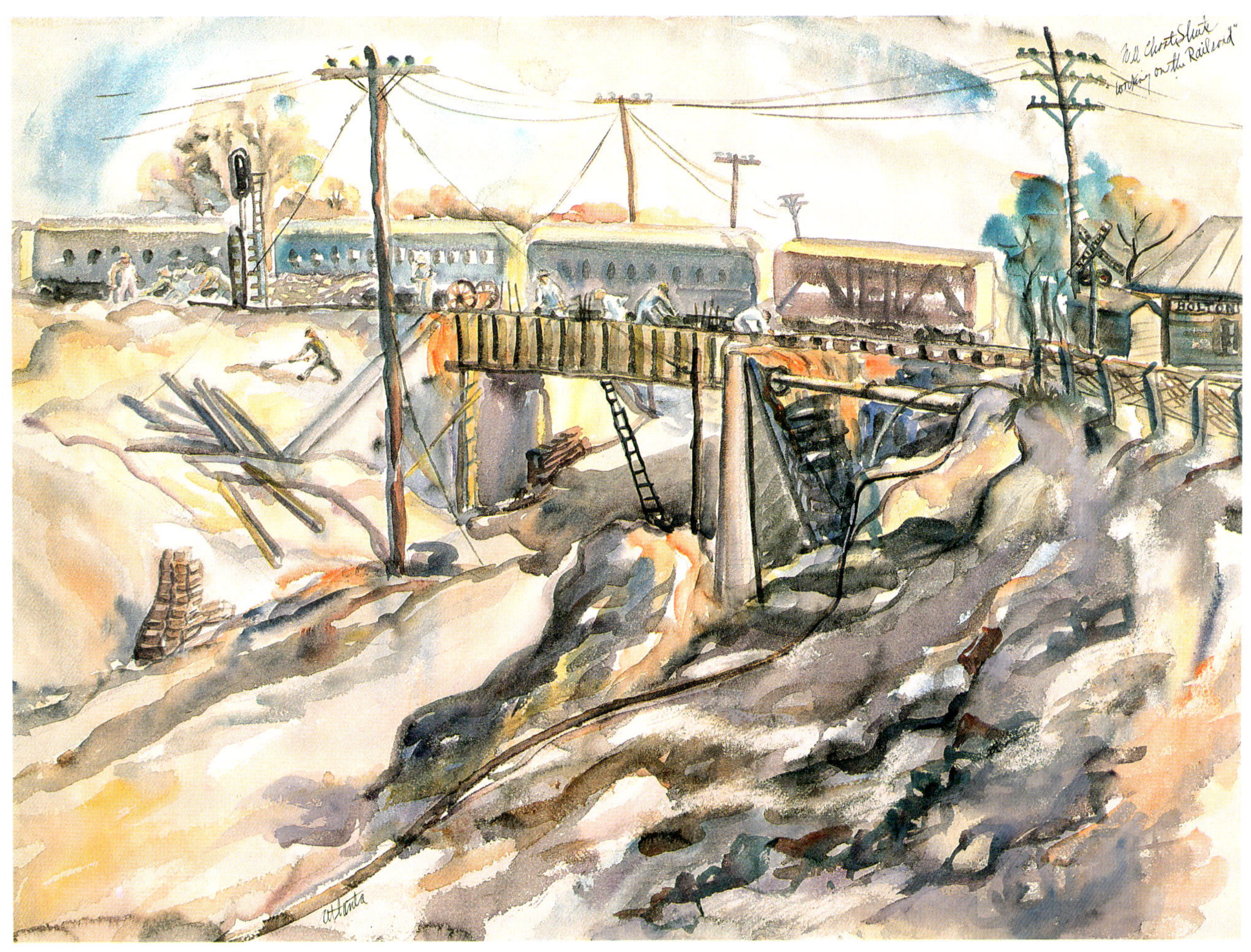
"We Casit Sliut"
Working on the Railroad
HOLTON
Atlanta

*Mary Flournoy
Passailaigue*

1908 – 1989

*Born, Columbus, Georgia; studied at Hollins College
in Virginia; and in various studio settings with
Edward Shorter, Dong Kingman, and Henry
Nordhausen; active in Columbus throughout her
career; died in Columbus.*

Carousel

1957

Watercolor on paper, 14 ½ x 21 ½ inches
1990.061

MARY PASSAILAIGUE'S PERSISTENT PURSUIT OF ARTISTIC STYLE
resulted in a variety of approaches to art, all enlivened by the merry
spirit for which she was known. Working from a large and
comfortable studio in the back yard of her home, "Tranquilla," in
Columbus, Georgia, Passailaigue had a career spanning some sixty
years, during which time she painted acutely representational
landscapes, watercolors in the oriental spirit, and highly keyed
watercolor observations of scenes abroad and closer to home.

One of the most important early infiuences in Passailaigue's life
was Edward Shorter, with whom she studied at a summer art colony
in North Carolina. Shorter eventually moved to Columbus and
became director of the Columbus Museum. Acknowledging his long-
term relationship with her, he noted in a brief exhibition catalog
essay, that they had "shared a mutual development through the
years."

Carousel is one of the artist's finest compositions, achieving a
kinetic sense of motion, while spanning the picture plane with bright
spots of color. The jolly expressions on the horses' faces make them
seem to be alive, a spirit altogether appropriate for the imaginary life
of those steeds frozen in place, upon whose backs legions of eager
children have leapt, ticket in hand, to ride and reach for the golden
ring.

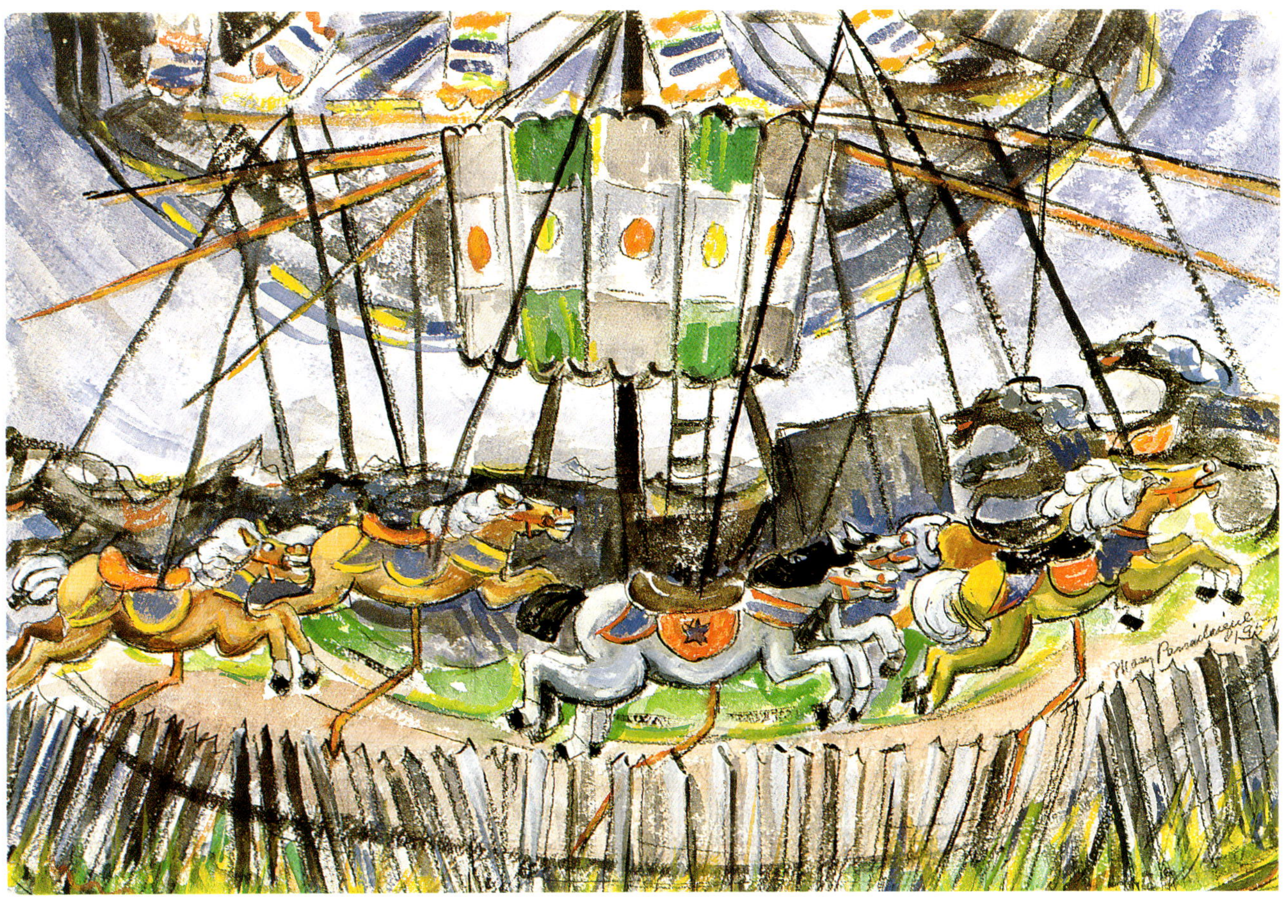

Benny Andrews

b.1930

Born, Madison, Georgia; B.F.A., The School of the Art Institute of Chicago, 1958; intermittent activity in the Madison, Georgia, area throughout his life.

Front Porch Conversation

1969

Ink on paper, 18 ⅛ x 23 ¾ inches
1993.C0623

BENNY ANDREWS HAS COMBINED A DISPARATE SET OF EXPERIENCES and circumstances into a cohesive formula for viewing the world around him. The child of sharecroppers, he grew up in rural Georgia, in a family whose visual and literary acumen is attested by the talents of his father, a self-taught painter; and his brother, a writer. But a strong undercurrent of the demands of his youth is always present in his work, for the thin life of rural poverty in the South is intertwined with his entire artistic vision.

Andrews was one of a handful of young talented black men who got out of the South in the 1950s and made the long trip "north, towards home" in the words of Willie Morris. He attended the University of Chicago and pursued an art degree in the prestigious Chicago Art Institute program, the same program which nurtured the talents of such other Southern artists as Roger Brown and Robert Gordy. After his graduation, he pursued his art and his commitment to black artists, becoming co-chair of the Black Emergency Cultural Coalition in the seminal year of 1968.

Front Porch Conversation has a fleeting quality, a fragile, tentative nature conveyed by the thin paper, the thin lines of the drawing. A visitor, leaning across the front porch rail, intent upon a visit, converses with a seated woman whose ease defines a sense of place further expanded by the very boards of the house itself. No single line of this work is wasted, no ambiguous shadows or tones convey a mood beyond the simple facts at hand. It is a work of intelligence and insight in which we are permitted to observe, but not to hear.

For the past twenty years, Andrews himself has been a careful observer of the American world around him. Feeling neither overwhelmed nor validated by life in America has proven a strength. In the catalog of his America series published by the New Jersey State Museum, he observed that, "this has been my existence in America all my life, betwixt and between, so those divisions I could take in stride. Somehow I've become immune to being over-loved and over-hated; therefore, I proudly cherish my sixty years of survival of still painting with pride befitting an individual who thrives in a world, America, that tolerates 'doing America his or her own way.'"

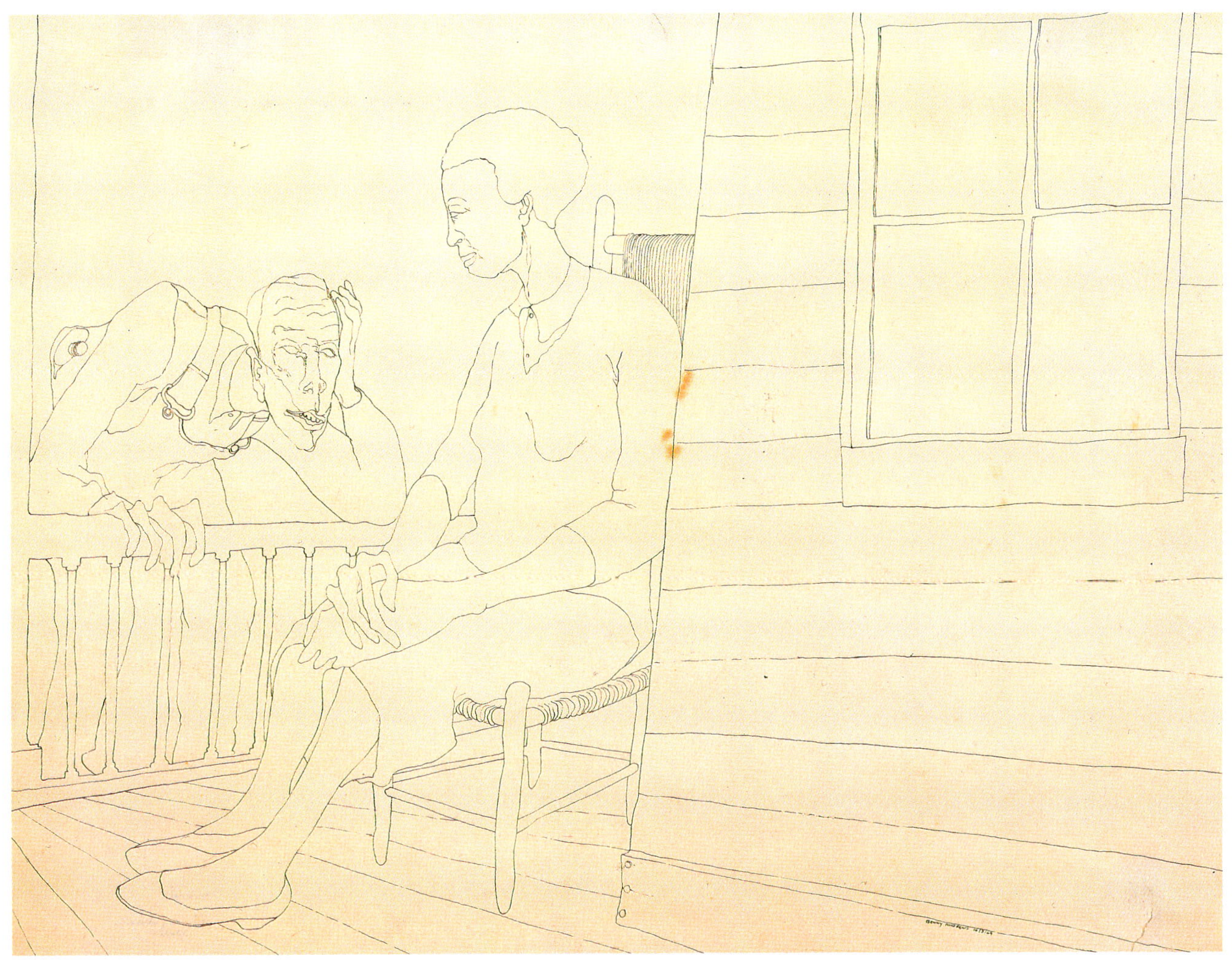

Myrtle Jones

b. 1913

Born, Forsyth County, Georgia, 1913; intermittent study with artists in Atlanta and Savannah; active in Savannah throughout her career.

Forsyth Park, Savannah

1967

Watercolor on paper, 17 ½ x 23 ¾ inches
1993.C0282

MYRTLE JONES IS PART OF THAT GREAT AND LENGTHY TRADITION OF women painters in Savannah that extends back to Emma Cheeves Wilkins in the first years of the century. Her biography notes that after her marriage, "she began to enroll in art courses offered at Savannah's colleges and museums. While this sketchy formal training was helpful, she began painting seriously on her own in 1950 and remains today a largely self-taught mistress of her metier."

While certainly not self-taught in the sense of contemporary rural visionary artists like Howard Finster or J. T. McCord, Jones does absorb several traditions in her work, notably that of impressionism. This she acknowledged in an interview with Sandi McDaniel for a Savannah newspaper, for she "likes soft colors . . . muted tones." She admires many of the more "vibrant painters" and often tries "their sharp angles, bold colors and clean lines. They paint all the way from the treble to the bass, so I do that, but then don't like it, and I paint over it."

In this watercolor, Jones has essayed a scene quite near her home, a rowhouse in the historic district of downtown Savannah. She achieves a true and sure grasp of place in this work, setting the splashing fountain deep within the grove of overarching trees which rise throughout the squares of the old city. Her palette is reminiscent of American impressionists like Maurice Prendergast and John Singer Sargent, whose decorative agenda supplanted the revolutionary color harmonics of their French counterparts.

It may be that Jones brings a peculiar sensitivity to Savannah reminiscent of that which Verner and Smith brought to Charleston. The two cities are close in time and space, disparate in atmosphere. Savannah dwells beneath the trees on ordered squares, at the end of a long river, back from the sea. Neither tourism nor development has greatly disturbed the architectural integrity which seems to moulder into the humid atmosphere with a gentle grace, rather than standing out in crisp restoration, like a well-conceived backdrop in an old South amusement park.

In her paintings and watercolors Jones may have grasped that quality as well as any artist who has ever worked in Savannah.

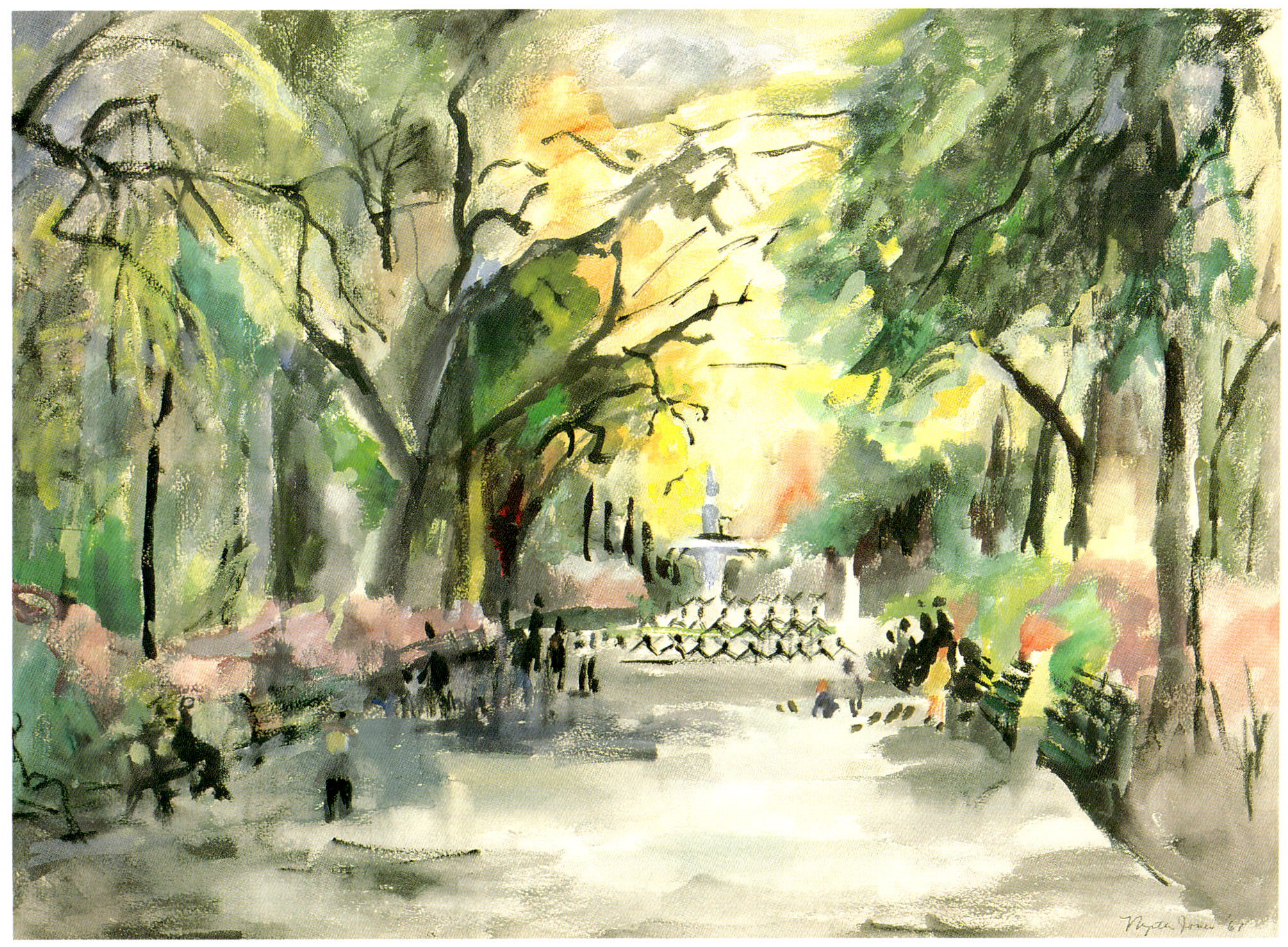

Robert Gordy

1933 – 1986

Born, Jefferson Island, Louisiana; M.F.A. Louisiana State University; active in New Orleans where he died.

Study for landscape with reclining figure

1980

Marker, ink and colored pencil on paper,
10½ x 11¼ inches
1992.001

BOB GORDY OFTEN NOTED, IN VARIOUS INTERVIEWS AND AUTO-biographical jottings, that the seminal event of his young life as an artist was viewing a work by Matisse at the Chicago Art Institute in 1955. *Bathers by the River* impressed the artist with its simplicity of vague, large lines outlining the figures, as well as the bold, forward presence of the leaves setting the scene.

"When I first thought of working with the figure, I was in college," he commented in a 1969 interview, "when everyone was painting like de Kooning." Preferring the figure, Gordy began to experiment with new approaches, returning to an oft-mentioned central figure, Cezanne. "I had a concern with the problem that everyone else is concerned with; how to paint on a flat surface after Cezanne."

Clearly the figural work of both Cezanne and Nicolas Poussin influenced Gordy to created flat, panoramic landscapes occupied by broadly outlined, and rather simplistic, figures of a symbolic, and indeed subliminally erotic, nature. Setting off those figures and the suggestive naturalistic elements of the landscape with lines was a unique innovation of the artist's, derived from his color sensibility. "I started doing this business of step up of (color) values – step up, step down, either in intensity of color or in light/dark."

Eventually the exacting nature, and implicit repetitive quality of this style provoked a genuine crisis of form for the artist. Following a major retrospective of the artist's work held at the New Orleans Museum of Art in 1981, he abandoned this style altogether, turning increasingly to more expressionistic works depicting large scale heads. This small drawing is a harbinger of things to come, a landscape of jagged edges outlining inert activity.

By deciding to live in the South, in New Orleans, Gordy felt that he was struggling against the mainstream, a decision which he determined had hurt his career. In an interview with William Fagaly of the New Orleans Museum of Art in 1976 he stated his notion of what it was to be Southern and an artist: "I do think there are some things that artists in the South seem to share – an interest in Surrealism, a wacky, oblique American version." Affirming the strong narrative tradition in the art of the South, he concluded, "There's also a lot of story-telling element, a sort of yarn quality. . ."

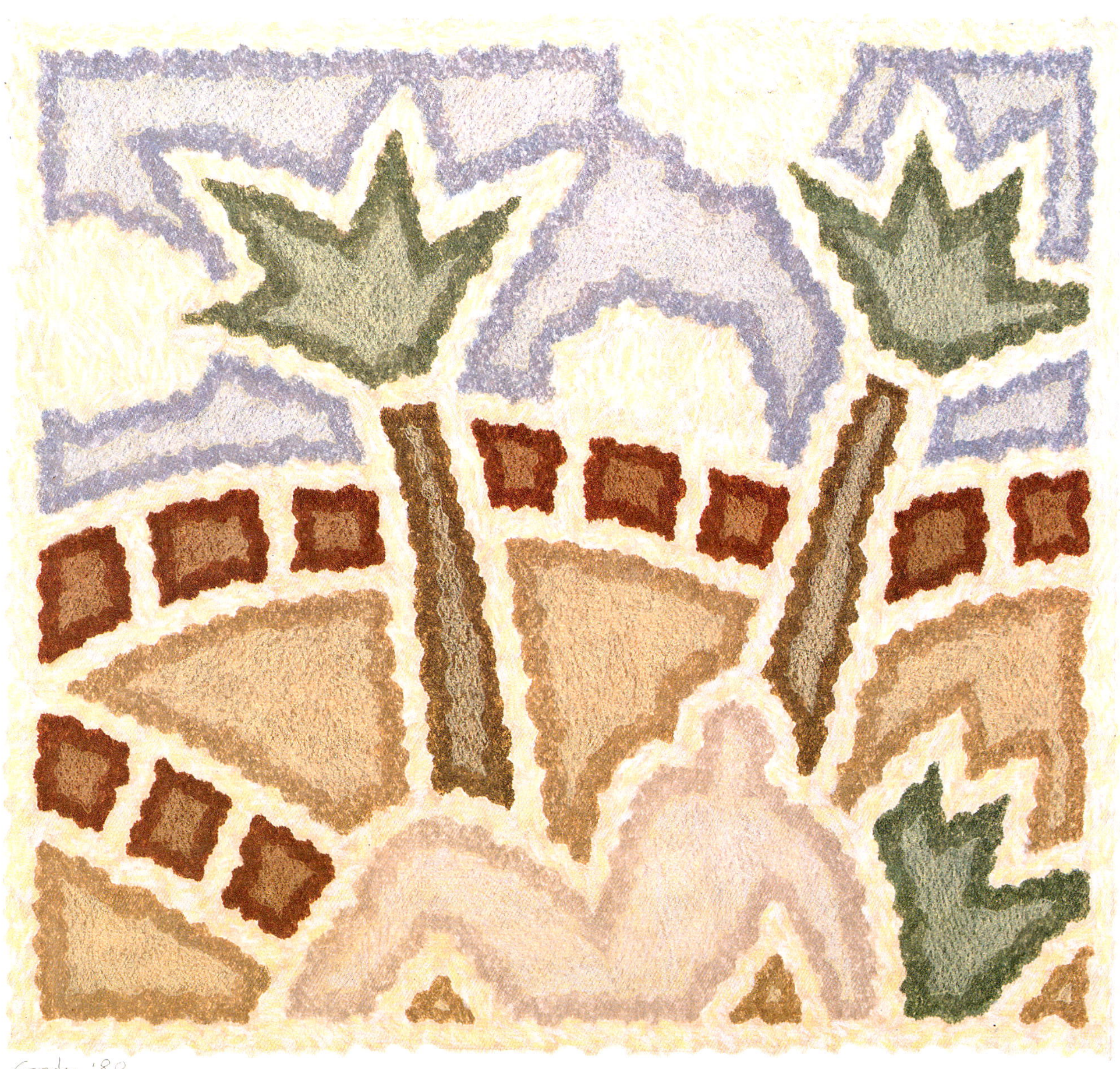

Herb Jackson

b. 1945

Born, Raleigh, North Carolina; B.A., Davidson College, 1967, M.F.A., University of North Carolina, 1970; active in North Carolina at Davidson College.

Abstraction – Blue and White

c. 1986

Acrylic on paper, 21¾ x 29¾ inches
1993.1104

A NATIVE SOUTHERNER, HERB JACKSON WAS EDUCATED IN THE SOUTH and has spent most of his career in North Carolina, teaching at Davidson College and building one of the finest small art departments in the region. While his art does not evince the same preoccupations with representation and narration that we have seen in previous works in this collection, it does share that warmth of coloration and unique personal vision which characterizes much of Southern art.

Jackson is still in league with those giants of abstract expressionism, Jackson Pollock and Franz Kline, in an age in which their large, splashy impenetrable canvases seem ever more remote. Non-objective art entered the South very slowly, seeping into the works of Will Henry Stevens and Paul Ninas in the more bohemian atmosphere of New Orleans long before it appeared on college campuses and in Peachtree Street galleries.

Undeterred, Jackson has quietly and persistently pursued an abstract venue. "I've always believed that if the work's good enough, if it's personal enough, and if my integrity remains intact, it will be seen," he commented to Richard Maschal in an article for *Southern Accents* magazine.

By mixing iridescent pigments into his surface, Jackson creates a mood of sparkle and shine which gives his work that elusive transcendental state that the best abstract works achieve. In his art, we are not so much concerned with looking into an implicit meaning, as we are entering a state of mind in which we are freed, and challenged to observe qualities previously unrevealed.

Writing of the evolution of the artist's style in 1988, the Southern art critic Donald Kuspit found great stylistic progress. "Every trace of preciousness and polish has been eliminated. The delicate rock of the surface has been split and shattered; its veins of color bleed violently. The paintings are as luminous as ever, but the light seems to vacillate in intensity more wildly than previously. It is more fitful, giving the pictorial terrain a new urgency."

This same sense of urgency, a sensitivity to the nuance of place, expanded by the gentle touch of light, dissolves in soft focus the inner visions of an artist working at the end of an ever lengthening tradition of the visual arts in the South.

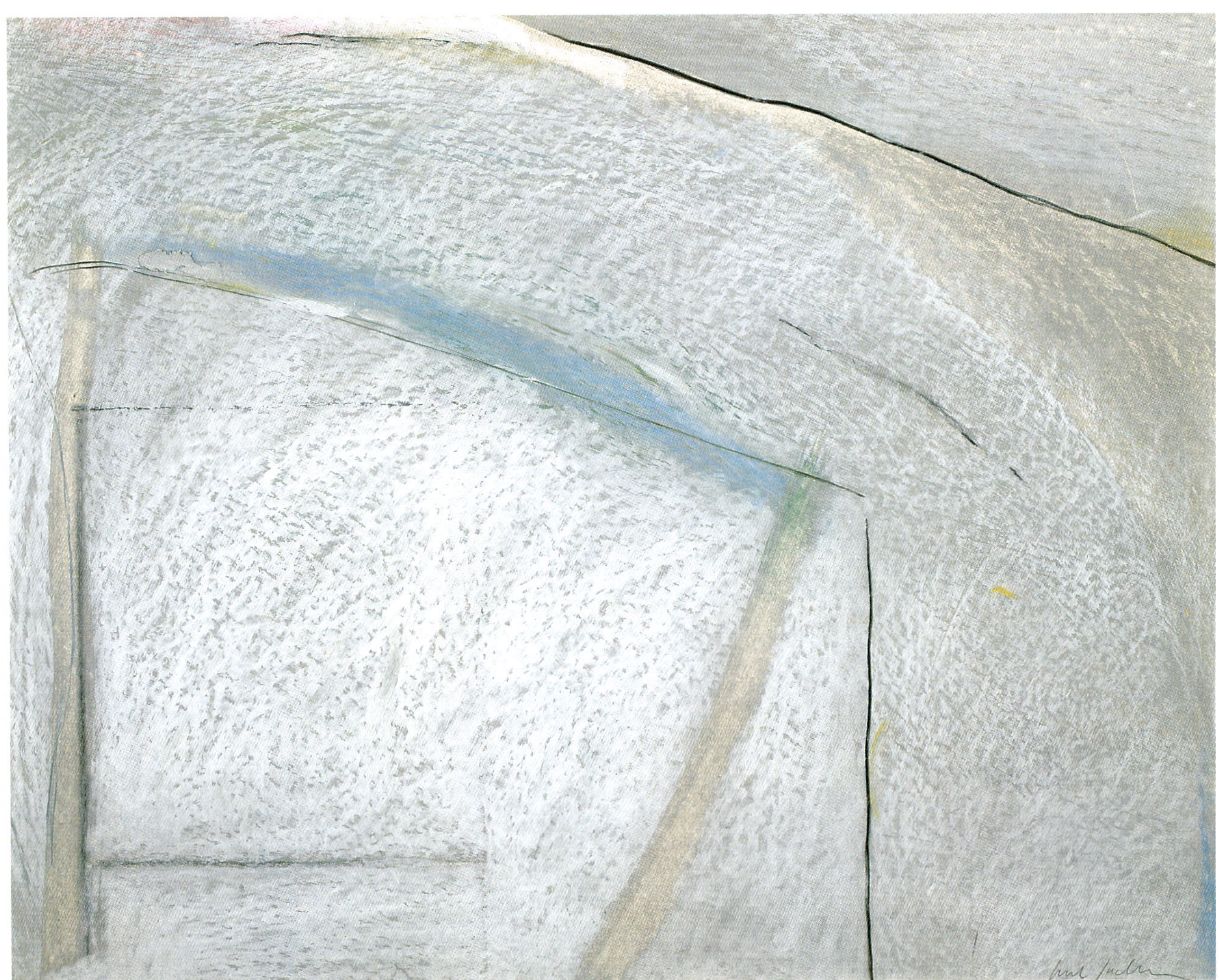

Lamar Dodd

b. 1909

Born, Fairburn, Georgia; studied, Georgia Institute of Technology, and with Boardman Robinson at the Art Students League, New York, 1928; active in Birmingham, Alabama, c. 1930-1937, and in Athens, Georgia since 1937.

Lobster Traps – Night No.1

1986

Watercolor on paper, 18⅛ x 24 inches
1987.1.3

LAMAR DODD HAS BEEN ONE OF THE MOST ARTICULATE AND influential academic artists of the South in the twentieth century. As chairman of the Fine Art Department of the University of Georgia he created, nurtured and sustained a faculty which has produced legions of successful and highly recognized artists over the last five decades.

Throughout that time Dodd also pursued his own art work, moving from the narrative representational style of the '30s into more experimental, non-objective forms during the heyday of abstract painting. Many of his experiments took him into cul-de-sacs terminating in derivation. Others, such as his series for the National Aeronautic and Space Administration and the open heart series, moved him on a course uncharted by any of his contemporaries.

His personal vision remained unchanged. Writing for the "College Art Journal", he asserted that "no art can be great unless the artist expresses with conviction, by means of his own personal skill and knowledge, both an idea and an emotion. As human beings it is our privilege to cultivate awareness – awareness in every center of human endeavor – yes awareness in art." Skill and knowledge were well chosen words, reminders of Dodd's relentless emphasis, as teacher and as painter, upon the skills essential to make, and to preserve, a work of art.

In 1986 Mary Dodd, the artist's wife of 56 years, died after several years of ill health. Seeking solace and renewal, he journeyed to Monhegan, Maine, a favorite retreat of long standing. There he could begin to create anew an astonishing late series of drawings, watercolors and pen and ink sketches. Once again his art transcends his craft in these intimate, sparkling epiphanies born out of ancient questions, alive with the skilled hand of an accomplished master in the late afternoon of a lengthy career.

Edmund Feldman, Dodd's longtime friend and colleague, sees the Monhegan works this way: "In his 'Lobster Pot' series, Dodd works out variations on the rectilinear grid, that much beloved scaffold of Cubist painting. However, Dodd insists on retaining the identifying forms of the lobster trap; he is reluctant to go the way of pure abstraction. The ropes, the netting, and the trap openings may look like notes on a musical staff, but their colors and textures smell of the sea."

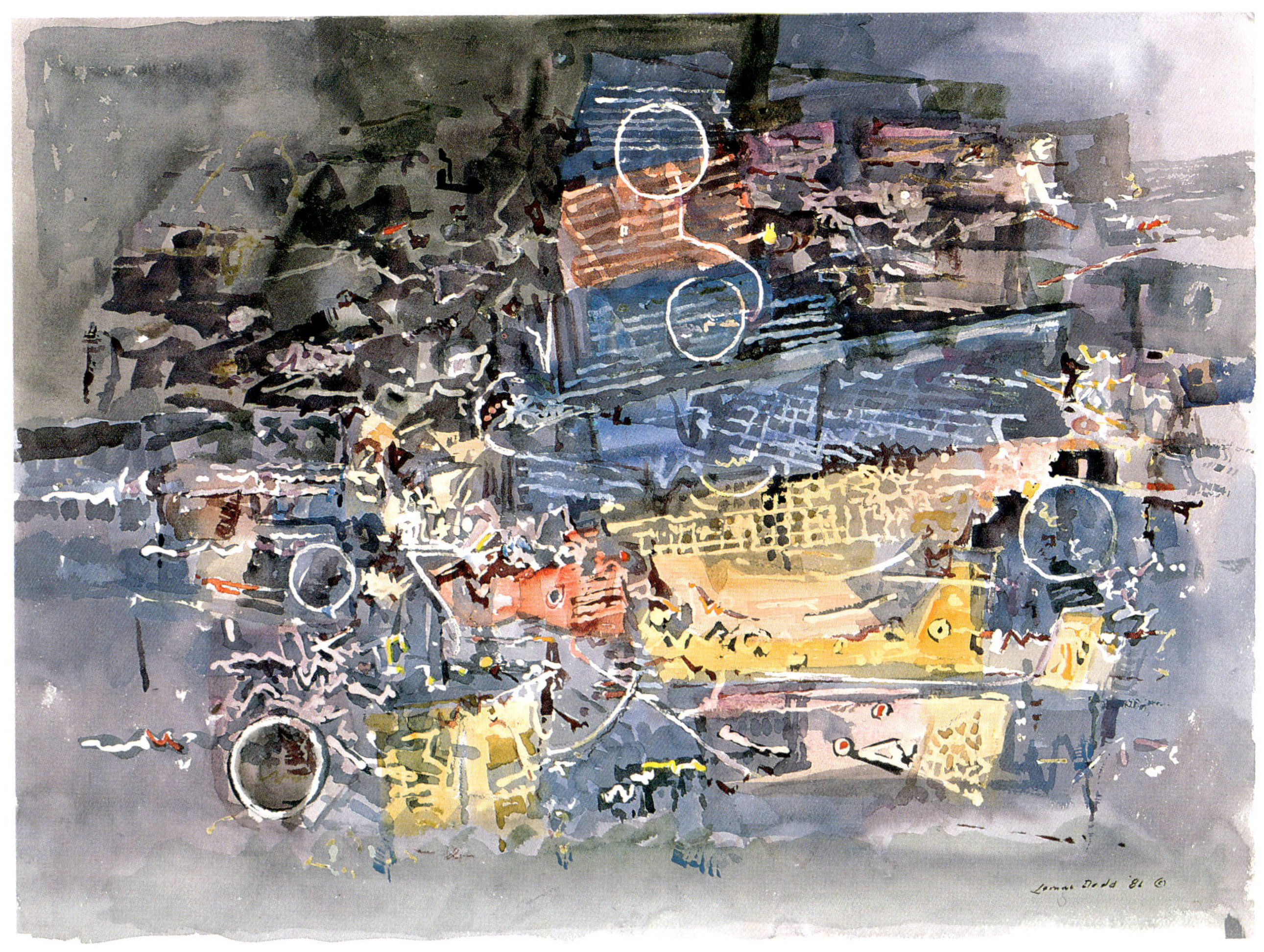

Select Bibliography

General Archival Sources

Center for the Study of Southern Painting, Morris Museum of Art, Augusta, Georgia. (all artists in this collection)

Historic New Orleans Collection, New Orleans, Louisiana. (all artists who have worked in Louisiana)

Smithsonian Institution Fine Arts Library, National Portrait Gallery, National Museum of American Art, Washington, D. C.

General Secondary Sources

Chambers, Bruce. *Art and Artists of the South.* Columbia, South Carolina, 1984.

Kelly, James. *The South on Paper.* Spartanburg, South Carolina, 1985.

Mahe, John A., II and Rosanne McCaffrey. *Encyclopedia of New Orleans Artists 1718-1918.* Historic New Orleans Collection, New Orleans, Louisiana, 1987.

Pennington, Estill Curtis. *A Southern Collection.* Morris Museum of Art, Augusta, Georgia, 1992.

Virginia Museum. *Painting in the South: 1564-1980.* Richmond, Virginia, 1983.

Sources, by Artist*

* LONGACRE, JAMES BARTON 1794−1869
Longacre, James Barton. "Excerpts from Longacre Diary for the year 1825." *Pennsylvania Magazine of History and Biography*, April, 1905.

Sadik, Marvin and Harold Francis Pfister. *American Portrait Drawings.* National Portrait Gallery, Smithsonian Institution, Washington, D.C., 1980.

Stewart, Robert Gordon. *A Nineteenth-Century Gallery of Distinguished Americans.* National Portrait Gallery, Smithsonian Institution, Washington, D.C., 1969.

* SULLY, GEORGE WASHINGTON 1816−1890
Ellsworth, Linda V. "George Washington Sully." *The Magazine Antiques*, March, 1983, pp. 600-605.

John C. Pace Library, Special Collections Division, University of West Florida, Pensacola.

* MEEKER, JOSEPH RUSLING 1827−1889
Barter, Judith., and Lynn G. Springer. *Currents of Expansion: Paintings in the Midwest*, 1820-1940. St. Louis Art Museum, 1977.

Brown, C. Reynolds. *Joseph Rusling Meeker: Images of the Mississippi Delta.* Montgomery Museum of Fine Arts, Montgomery, Alabama, 1981.

Meeker, Joseph Rusling. "Opening Address at the St. Louis Art Society Annual Meeting." *The Western*, December, 1878.

_____. "Some Accounts of the Old and New Masters." *The Western.* n.d., 1878.

Pennington, Estill Curtis. *Look Away: Reality and Sentiment in Southern Art.* Atlanta, Georgia, 1989.

* KEY, JOHN ROSS 1837−1920
Harrison, Alfred C., Jr. "Bierstadt's 'Bombardment of Fort Sumter' Reattributed." *The Magazine Antiques*, February, 1986.

* WILSON, ROBERT BURNS 1850−1916
Coleman, J. Winston. *Robert Burns Wilson.* Lexington, Kentucky, 1956.

Jones, Arthur F. and Bruce Weber. *The Kentucky Painter from the Frontier Era to the Great War.* University of Kentucky Art Museum, Lexington, 1981.

Ward, William S. *A Literary History of Kentucky.* University of Tennessee Press, Knoxville, 1988.

* WOODWARD, ELLSWORTH 1861−1939
Barkemeyer, Estelle. *Ellsworth Woodward: His Life and Work.* Unpublished master's thesis, Tulane University, New Orleans, 1942.

Cullison, William R. III. *Two Southern Impressionists: An Exhibition of the Work of the Woodward Brothers.* Tulane University Art Collection, 1984.

Howard Tilton Memorial Library, Special Collections, Tulane University, New Orleans, Louisiana.

Ormonde, Suzanne and Mary E. Irvine. *Louisiana's Art Nouveau: The Crafts of the Newcomb Style.* Gretna, Louisiana, 1976.

Pennington, Estill Curtis. *Downriver: Currents of Style in Louisiana Painting 1800-1950.* Gretna, Louisiana, 1991.

Poesch, Jessie. *Newcomb Pottery: An Enterprise for Southern Women,* 1895-1940. Exton, Pennsylvania, 1984.

Works Progress Administration Papers, New Orleans Museum of Art. (contains manuscript copies of major lectures and articles on art education delivered by Woodward during the 1930s.)

* HOLMES, WILLIAM HENRY 1846−1933
Goetzmann, William H. "Limner of Grandeur: William H. Holmes." *The American West XV*, May/June, 1978.

_____. *William H. Holmes: Panoramic Artist.* Amon Carter Museum of Art, Fort Worth, Texas, 1977.

Holmes, William Henry. *Random Records of a Lifetime, 1846-1931. . . in XX Volumes.* Smithsonian Institution Fine Arts Library, National Portrait Gallery, National Museum of American Art, Washington.

Pennington, Estill Curtis. *Downriver: Currents of Style in Louisiana Art 1800-1950.* Gretna, Louisiana, 1991.

Nelson, Clifford M. "William Henry Holmes: Beginning a Career in Art and Science." *Records of the Columbia Historical Society, Washington, D.C., the Fiftieth Volume.* University of Virginia Press, 1980.

Smithsonian Institution Archives, Washington, D.C.

* BURCHFIELD, CHARLES 1893−1967
Baur, John I. H. *The Inlander: Life and Work of Charles Burchfield, 1893-1967.* University of Delaware Press, 1982.

* LEIGH, WILLIAM ROBINSON 1866−1955
Dubois, June. "The Paintings of W. R. Leigh: Sane, Honest and Competent." *American Art & Antiques*, November/December, 1978, pp. 102-109.

Leigh, William Robinson. *Frontiers of Enchantment.* New York, 1938.

_____. *The Western Pony*. New York, 1933.

Rio Grande Historical Collections, New Mexico State University, Los Cruces, New Mexico, William R. Leigh correspondence with A. N. Blazer, March 1931-January, 1935.

* SMITH, ALICE RAVENEL HUGER 1876–1958
Alice Ravenel Huger Smith: An Appreciation on the Occasion of Her Eightieth Birthday, from her Friends. Charleston, South Carolina, 1956.

Severens, Martha. "Lady of the Low Country." *South Carolina Wildlife*, March-April, 1979.

_____. "Reveries: The Work of Alice Ravenel Huger Smith." *Art Voices South I*, January-February, 1978.

_____. *Alice Ravenel Huger Smith: An Artist, A Place and A Time*. Carolina Art Association/Gibbes Museum of Art. Charleston, South Carolina, 1993.

Smith, Alice Ravenel Huger. *A Charleston Sketchbook 1796-1806. . .* Carolina Art Association, Charleston, 1940.

* IRVINE, SARAH AGNES ESTELLE 1887–1970
Blasberg, Robert W. "The Sadie Irvine Letters: A Further Note on the Production of Newcomb Pottery." *The Magazine Antiques*, August, 1971, pp. 250-251.

Ormonde, Suzanne and Mary E. Irvine. *Louisiana's Art Nouveau: The Crafts of the Newcomb Style*. Gretna, Louisiana, 1976.

Poesch, Jessie. *Newcomb Pottery: An Enterprise for Southern Women*, 1895-1940. Exton, Pennsylvania, 1984.

* BELL, WENONAH DAY 1890–1981
Bell, Wenonah Day. *The Restless Bells*. New York, 1973.

Greenville County Museum of Art. *Work Song*. Greenville, South Carolina, 1990.

* MURPHY, CHRISTOPHER P. H. 1869–1939
Shellman, Feay. *Christopher P. H. Murphy 1869-1939: A Retrospective*. Telfair Academy of Arts and Sciences, Savannah, Georgia, 1985.

Telfair Academy of Arts and Sciences, Savannah, Georgia, artist's files.

* GREGORY, ANGELA 1903–1990
Artist's files, New Orleans Museum of Art.

Lamantia, James. "Angela Gregory." Ephemeral exhibition catalog, New Orleans, 1989.

Works Progress Administration Papers, New Orleans Museum of Art.

* HARLESTON, EDWIN AUGUSTUS 1882–1931
Gibbes Museum of Art, artist's files.

Igoe, Lynn Moody and James Igoe. *250 Years of Afro-American Art, An Annotated Bibliography*. New York, 1981.

Reynolds, Gary A. and Beryle J. Wright. *Against the Odds: African-American Artists and the Harmon Foundation*. The Newark Museum, Newark, New Jersey, 1989.

* HERGESHEIMER, ELLA SOPHONISBA 1873–1943
Burton, Vincent. "Some Portraits by Ella S. Hergesheimer." *International Studio*, 37, March, 1909.

Kelly, James C. "Landscape and Genre Painting in Tennessee, 1810-1985." *Tennessee Historical Quarterly*, 44, no. 2, Summer, 1985.

Nashville Banner. July 5, 1932, and February 21, 1938.

* HUTTY, ALFRED 1877–1954
Gibbes Art Gallery. *Alfred Hutty: A Memorial Exhibition*. Carolina Art Association, Charleston, South Carolina, 1956.

Harrison, Birge. "Old Charleston As Pictured by Alfred Hutty." *The American Magazine of Art*, 192?.

Phillips, Duncan. "Alfred Hutty." *American Etchers*, Vol. II, New York, 1929.

Saunders, Boyd, and Ann McAden. *Alfred Hutty and the Charleston Renaissance*. Orangeburg, South Carolina, 1991.

* NINAS, PAUL 1903–1964
Early, Eleanor. "Gave Up the Most Beautiful Model in Paris for Art on a Tropic Isle." *Every Week* magazine, 1930.

Heintzen, Harry. "Meet the Pilot of Flight to Fancy." *The Times-Picayune/New Orleans States Item* magazine, October 19, 1947.

Orillion, Kathleen. *Paul Ninas 1903-1964*. Louisiana Arts and Sciences Center, Baton Rouge, 1986.

Eaves, James M. ed. *Memoranda on the Life and Work of Ms. Elizabeth White*. Unpublished manuscript, Sumter, South Carolina, 1986.

Greenville County Museum of Art. *Work Song*. Greenville, South Carolina, 1990.

Parris, Nina. *South Carolina Collection 1770-1985*. The Columbia Museum, Columbia, South Carolina, 1985.

Sumter Museum of Art, artist's files.

* WHITE, ELIZABETH 1883–1976
Columbia Museum of Art. *Elizabeth White. . . a retrospective exhibition of Southern creative arts. . .* Columbia, South Carolina, 1957.

* JONES, NELL CHOATE 1879–1981
"Confederate's Daughter Returns Home for Visit." *Hawkinsville Dispatch & News*, January 3, 1979.

* RIPLEY, AIDEN LASSELL 1896–1969
Coe Kerr Gallery. *Aiden Lassell Ripley 1896-1969 Watercolors*. New York, 1982.

Cohen, Stephen D. "Aiden Lassell Ripley: American Painter, 1896 - 1969." Unpublished typescript, cited by Kelly in *The South on Paper*, as being in the Smithsonian Fine Arts Library, and now likely to be in the Archives of American Art.

Howlett, Roger D. "Aiden Lassell Ripley." *Childs Gallery Bulletin*, II, Winter-Spring, 1984.

Perera, Guido. *Aiden Lassell Ripley, Sporting Etchings*. Barre, Massachusetts, 1970.

Weeks, Edward. *A. Lassell Ripley, Paintings*. Boston, Massachusetts, 1972.

✳ BROOK, ALEXANDER 1898–1980
Kelly, A. W. *A Retrospective Exhibition of Paintings by Alex Brook 1898-1980.* Salander-O'Reilly Art Gallery, New York, 1982.

King, Alma S. *Alexander Brook (1898-1980): Looking Back.* Santa Fe East Gallery, Santa Fe, New Mexico, 1981.

✳ VERNER, ELIZABETH O'NEILL 1883–1979
Gibbes Gallery of Art. *Elizabeth O'Neill Verner, A retrospective on her Eightieth Birthday.* Carolina Art Association, Charleston, South Carolina, 1964.

Greenville County Museum of Art. *Work Song.* Greenville, South Carolina, 1990.

Saunders, Boyd. *Mirror of Time, Elizabeth O'Neill Verner's Charleston.* McKissick Museums, The University of South Carolina, Columbia, South Carolina, 1983.

Verner, Elizabeth O'Neill. *Mellowed by Time, A Charleston Notebook.* Charleston, South Carolina, 1970.

__________. *Prints and Impressions of Charleston.* Columbia, South Carolina, c. 1940.

✳ McCRADY, JOHN 1911–1968
Marshall, Keith. *John McCrady 1911-1968.* New Orleans Museum of Art, 1975.

McCrady, John, Caroline Durieux, and Ralph Wickiser. *Mardi Gras Day.* New Orleans, 1948.

McCrady Papers, Mrs. John McCrady, New Orleans.

Pennington, Estill Curtis. *Downriver: Currents of Style in Louisiana Painting 1800-1950.* Gretna, Louisiana, 1991.

Summers, Marion. "Studies in Contrast: Chauvinism and Truth." *The Daily Worker,* May 29, 1946.

✳ PITTMAN, HOBSON 1900–1972
Hull, William. *The World of Hobson Pittman.* University of Pennsylvania State Museum of Art, University Park, 1972.

Turner, Evan. *Hobson Pittman, Retrospective Exhibition: His Work since 1920.* North Carolina Museum of Art, Raleigh, 1963.

✳ LEMM, ADELE 1904–1977
Alice Bingham Gallery artist's files, Memphis, Tennessee.

Brooks Memorial Art Gallery. *Recent Oils and Pastels by Adele Lemm.* Memphis, Tennessee, 1956.

"Art Exhibition Notes." *New York Herald Tribune,* February 6, 1960.

Northrop, Guy. "Lemm Style Works Its Charm." *Memphis Commercial Appeal,* nd. (late 60s).

✳ PASSAILAIGUE, MARY FLOURNOY 1908–1989
Fussell, Fred C. *Mary Flournoy Passailaigue.* Columbus Museum, Columbus, Georgia, 1990.

Shorter, Edward. *Mary Passailaigue.* Columbus Museum, Columbus, Georgia, nd.

✳ ANDREWS, BENNY 1930
Alloway, Lawrence. *Benny Andrews: The Bicentennial Series.* High Museum of Art, Atlanta, 1975.

Andrews, Benny. "Becoming Professional." *American Artist,* January, 1990.

__________. *Between the Lines: Seventy Drawings and Seven Essays.* New York, 1978.

__________. "Decentralization: The Greening of America." *Art Papers,* March/April, 1986.

Bladon, Patricia P. *Folk – The Art of Benny and George Andrews.* Memphis Brooks Museum of Art, Memphis, Tennessee, 1990.

Cederholm, Theresa D. *Afro-American Artists: A Bio-bibliographical Directory.* Boston, Massachusetts, 1973.

Igoe, Lynn Moody and James Igoe. *250 Years of Afro-American Art, An Annotated Bibliography.* New York, 1981.

Livingston, Jane and John Beardsley. *Black Folk Art in America 1930-1980.* Corcoran Gallery of Art, Washington, D.C., 1982.

Rivera, George, Benny Andrews, et. al. *Benny Andrews: The America Series.* The Triton Museum of Art, Santa Clara, California, 1992.

✳ GORDY, ROBERT 1933–1986
Adams, Franklin. "An Interview with Robert Gordy." *Les Beaux Arts.* New Orleans, c. 1985.

Baro, Gene. *Robert Gordy: Paintings and Drawings. 1960-1980.* New Orleans Museum of Art, 1981.

Fagaly, William. "Robert Gordy." *Art in America,* July-August, 1976, pp. 78-79.

Walker, Barry. *Robert Gordy.* University of South Florida Galleries, Tampa, 1985.

✳ JACKSON, HERB 1945
Kuspit, Donald. *Herb Jackson: Dream of the Minotaur.* Phyllis Weil & Company, New York, 1988.

✳ DODD, LAMAR 1909
Collier, Graham. "Lamar Dodd: Serene and Clear," *American Artist.* June, 1980.

David Ramus Ltd. *Lamar Dodd: Monhegan Watercolors.* Atlanta, Georgia, 1987.

Evans, Gary. "A Lion in Winter," *Athens Magazine,* Spring, 1989.

Georgia Museum of Art, Athens, Georgia. Artist's files.

High Museum of Art in collaboration with the Georgia Museum of Art. *Lamar Dodd: A Retrospective Exhibition.* University of Georgia Press, 1970.

Index of Artists Illustrated

⌈A Note on the Types⌉

The types used in *Light Of Touch* are representative of the evolution
and convergence of several trends in British type design during the
late eighteenth and early nineteenth centuries. The principal text type
is Bell, a revival of the fine transitional letter cut by Richard Austin
for the publisher John Bell in 1788, produced under the direction of
Stanley Morison & Frank H. Pierpont for the Monotype Corporation
in 1930. The script type is Young Baroque, designed by Doyle Young
for Esselte-Letraset in 1989, an exemplar of the scripts called *anglais*
which were made taking the widely-used running hand of English
commerce as a model. The square-serif used for the titles of the works
on paper is Egyptian Extended and the sans serif used for information
relating to the works is Bureau Grotesque No.53. Both of these styles
of type first appeared in the catalogues of several English foundries in
the early 1800s and are reflective, on the one hand, of the period
fascination with the art and architecture of Egyptian Antiquity and,
on the other, of the developing mechanical aesthetic of an industrial
society. Egyptian Extended was released by Monotype in the 1920s;
Bureau Grotesque No.53 is one of a series of such types drawn by
David Berlow – after the designs of the Stephenson Blake Foundry –
and released by The Font Bureau in 1990.